CAFE HOPPING in the SOUTHWEST

CAFE HOPPING in the SOUTHWEST

100 Charming Places to Eat
Plus Tips for Tourists

Sunny Conley

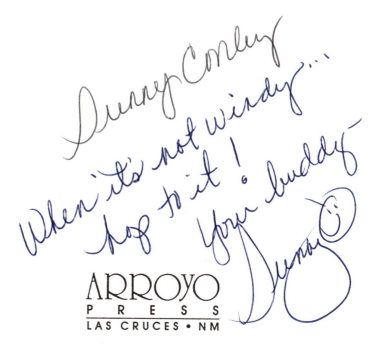

Sunny Conley
When it's not windy...
hop to it!
your buddy

ARROYO
P R E S S
LAS CRUCES • NM

Published by
Arroyo Press
P.O. Box 4333
Las Cruces, NM 88003
(505) 522-2348

Printed in the United States of America

Library of Congress Cataloging in Publication Data Available

The cover design is based in part on an Alexander Henry fabric. Reprinted by permission of Alexander Henry Fabrics, Inc., Los Angeles.

Author photo by Tonya A. Evatt. Fashions courtesy of Outlaws, Las Cruces, New Mexico. Jewelry courtesy of Silver Assets, Mesilla, New Mexico.

To Ed, my compeer
"It's just like the CIA at lunch time."

CONTENTS

Contents

Contents

FOREWORD

The real flavor of the Southwest lies in its authentic cooking, which often can be found only at those cafes known to the local inhabitants. So when you're traveling this vast region, avoid the fast food dispensaries and those fuel-stop, prepackaged sandwiches. Instead, taste some of the truly delightful dishes found in these one-of-a-kind restaurants and cafes.

Whether you're in the mood for the best chicken enchiladas north of the border, juicy buffalo steaks, double-fisted-double-cheeseburgers dressed with fiery chile, or ribs smothered with a chin-dripping barbecue sauce, *Cafe Hopping in the Southwest* is your concise guide.

After you've satisfied your hunger pangs, author Sunny Conley offers tips on what to see and do in each locale. If you just want to kick back in the Pinos Altos Wilderness in New Mexico, tour the winding streets of historic Jerome in Arizona or chug across the steep Colorado border on the historic Cumbres and

Toltec Mountain Railroad, this book will spice up your travels.

Join Sunny in her quest for those cafes that epitomize the spirit of our remarkable, exciting and colorful Southwest.

LYNN NUSOM

Lynn Nusom is a food editor, book reviewer and the author of several Southwestern cookbooks, including *Christmas in New Mexico*, *The New Mexico Cookbook* and *The Sizzling Southwestern Cookbook*.

PREFACE

My public food adventures began in 1990 when I entered the Holiday Cookbook Contest sponsored by the local newspaper, the *Las Cruces Sun-News*. I placed second with "Sunny's Salsa." Two years later, I was invited by *Sun-News* Editor Harold Cousland to write the city's first weekly restaurant review, "The Palate Patrol." Since then, I have reviewed nearly 200 restaurants in Southern New Mexico and El Paso, Texas.

The idea for *Cafe Hopping in the Southwest* was sparked by a reader who expressed how she enjoyed reading about the little known and out-of-the-way restaurants I had featured in my column. Initially, I planned the book to include New Mexico cafes exclusively. But while on a trek in Arizona, I happened upon several unique cafes near the New Mexico border. Perhaps, I thought, I'd include just a few of these. But the farther I traveled into the Arizona heartland, the more cafes I found — places I believed tourists would enjoy as much as I. These too, I reasoned, *must* be included in the book.

Then a fellow Arizona traveler asked if I planned to include California cafes. When I answered no, he said, "Too bad, there's this little Mexican place in Blythe, just across the state line, I know you'd love." Two days later, I was noshing chips dipped into homemade salsa at Amapola's Cafe located in, you guessed it, Blythe.

The cafes found in the bordering regions of Colorado, Texas, and Palomas, Mexico were "discovered" similarly with the help of some locals, a little luck, and a lot of driving. In all, I traveled 8,000 miles, sampled the offerings of more than 100 cafes, and made some wonderful new friends — many of whom you'll meet when you too visit these charming cafes that reflect — How the Southwest was Yum.

INTRODUCTION

E xperience the Southwest. Not just the sites but also the cuisine — the chile-charged burgers, the salmon drenched in chipotle sauce, the cornhusk-wrapped tamales, or just plain, good old-fashioned eats. Goodies like these can't be found in touristy fast food joints and restaurants. They can be discovered only in ma and pa cafes, charming places often passed up in favor of familiar but ordinary restaurants.

The cafes are grouped by state, then in alphabetical order by city and name of restaurant. Each profile highlights one or more aspects of the cafe's character that makes it unique. That could be its history, its owners, its chef, or its cuisine.

Although prices are not noted, expect to spend about $6. Some cafes may cost more but these have been included because of their outstanding cuisine.

To help in planning your itinerary, profiles also highlight area attractions within about an hour's drive. An index, locator map, and a glossary are also included. Use this guide to supplement other tourist literature, specifically detailed state maps.

The proverbial laid-back Southwest lifestyle takes many forms — the odd hours, for example, that many cafe owners keep. Some are open only for breakfast and lunch, or for lunch and dinner. Although it's seldom the case, others may close for the season, be it summer or winter. And it's not uncommon for hard-working cafe owners and managers to lower the blinds for an afternoon *siesta*. Such "nap" times vary also. Call first before venturing too far out of your way.

The author invites cafe hoppers to share their comments, impressions and suggestions by using the feedback form located in the back of the book.

There is no love sincerer than the love of food.
George Bernard Shaw

Locations are approximate.

Locations are approximate.

ARIZONA

Arizona remains one of the Southwest's most popular retreats. In winter, snowbirds take advantage of the southern valleys' near ideal weather — sunny skies, low humidity, and mild temperatures. In summer, when the sun blisters the valleys, natives beeline north to find reprieve within the grassy headlands and mountain rises draped with juniper, oak, piñon, pine and fir.

Arizona is nicknamed the Grand Canyon State for good reason. Each year, a million tourists, representing every point on the globe, experience this unrivaled natural wonder. Adventurous spirits hike the rim paths or bravely descend the torturous trail to the canyon floor.

A playland for all sports and outdoor enthusiasts, Arizona also beckons artists, museum-hoppers, and big city shoppers. Discover Arizona's rich history by exploring its old mining towns, Indian reservations, missions, parks and monuments.

18 STEPS
51 Main Street
Bisbee, AZ
(520) 432-5155

SPECIALTIES
Homemade
soups, salads,
sandwiches,
desserts

AREA ATTRACTIONS
Douglas,
Tombstone,
Chiricahua
National
Monument,
Tubac, Nogales,
AZ; Agua Prieta,
Mex.

Not long ago, patrons were required to climb 18 stairs to the entrance of 18 Steps. But no longer. Owners Joe and Natalie Frederickson moved the cafe to a new, lower location. Now, the tiny, seven-table cafe, dressed in a striped awning, is at street level.

It's just one of nearly a dozen food houses that line Bisbee's busy Main Street. But locals (I asked more than 20) seem to prefer 18 Steps' homemade savories best. Chef Joe prepares Big Lox Salads sprinkled with capers. His pasta carbonara features noodles and piquant sausage tossed in a cream 'n eggs sauce. My favorite is the spanakopita, a phyllo dough "sandwich" stuffed with sautéed spinach and onions. Then there are Natalie's desserts, especially her mousse, which one of her regular customers claims "is to die for."

Hillside-clinging Bisbee, swallowed by the Mule Mountains, was once a copper mining town. Today, it's a shopper's haven. Take a tour of the old Copper Queen Mine, itself a trip back in time.

Naming restaurants after amphibians has become a habit for Ed Chilleen. In the early '80s, for example, he opened the Horny Toad, which he later sold. Now he's proprietor of the Satisfied Frog, so named (I'm told) when one of Ed's pals said, "I'd rather be a satisfied frog than a horny toad." Ed and wife Marie also own the cantina and microbrewery located adjacent to the Frog. Crazy Ed's Original Chile Beer, garnished with a plump, snappy-green chile, is a hit in the U.S. and Japan.

The restaurant, with lovely patios and a beer garden, is outfitted Western-style, circa 1880s. Knotty pine dresses walls, wood shavings dust floors, gingham cloths and kerosene lanterns decorate tables, and life-size Indian mannequins pose casually on steps.

Homemade's the word — from the breads to the smoked-in-house meats. I sampled Ed's heavenly chili heaped in a sourdough bread bowl and the "man-size" Reuben — quality corned beef piled high on rye-rich, butter-moistened bread. Exceptional.

On a budget? Watch out! Shops abound in Cave Creek. Visit Cave Creek Museum.

SATISFIED FROG SALOON & RESTAURANT

Frontier
Town Mall
Cave Creek, AZ
(602) 253-FROG

SPECIALTIES
Reuben
sandwiches,
sourdough bread
chili bowl,
hamburgers

AREA ATTRACTIONS
Pioneer Arizona
Living History
Museum,
Plotkin Judaica
Museum,
Phoenix, AZ

WHEELER INN CAFE

Main Street
Chloride, AZ
(520) 565-9608

SPECIALTIES

Burgers, "boiled first" fries, meatloaf, mashed potatoes and gravy

AREA ATTRACTIONS

Lake Mohave, Lake Mead, Hoover Dam, AZ; Laughlin, NV

About five miles east of Grasshopper Junction on U.S. 93 rests the old mining town of Chloride, founded in 1862. After the mine closed in the mid '40s, few people stayed on. But others — artists, business people, retirees — were attracted to Chloride's laid-back lifestyle. Today, the tiny town boasts a population of 300, many of whom dine at Dennis and Mary Wheeler's bar and restaurant, the Wheeler Inn Cafe.

Swinging doors lead from the Western-style bar to the cafe strung with Christmas tree lights. The cafe is known for its chubby, juicy burgers, and "boiled first," says waitress Jo D'Angelo, homemade fries. Other kitchen-conjured specialties include meatloaf, teriyaki chicken and old-fashioned, buttery, mashed potatoes and gravy.

Chloride artists sell and show their work in studios and shops. Entertainment includes Gay '90s melodramas, in which, Jo says, she often participates. Saturday afternoons are reserved for the Vaudeville Troop at the Town Hall. Visit the oldest regularly operated post office in Arizona, the Jim Fritz Museum, and the town's original jailhouse.

Travelers headed north on Highway 89 toward Prescott often turn off at the giant saguaro that marks the road to Congress, a small, gold mining town established in 1870. Modern-day miners rise early for breakfast at Cafe Arizona, an Old West style cafe with a functional, modern outhouse out back. The cafe is owned by former South Africans Simon Smith and his wife, Janet Palmer, who arrived in America just over 10 years ago. They lived in Florida briefly, but after viewing the film, *Baghdad Cafe*, the couple was inspired to pack their bags and head to the Southwest to open a diner.

Menu items change seasonally — more salads are offered in the summer. According to Simon, he and Janet do most of the cooking. "We're best known for our hamburgers, including The Vegetarian." Also popular are guacamole, Mexican quesadillas, chimichangas and buffalo chicken wings. Thirty kinds of imported and domestic beer are featured.

Congress passers-through are awe-struck by the miles and miles of surrounding desertland. Travelers often visit nearby Stanton to tour the old opera house, stage stop, hotel, and gold mining shanties.

CAFE ARIZONA
201 Highway 71
Congress, AZ
(520) 427-6331

SPECIALTIES
Hamburgers, chicken wings, quesadillas, chimichangas

AREA ATTRACTIONS
Wickenberg, Prescott, Jerome

MIKE & DEE'S RESTAURANT

Pierce Ferry Road
Dolan Springs, AZ
(520) 767-4777

SPECIALTIES

Pizza, Mexican
plates

AREA ATTRACTIONS

Lake Mead,
Lake Havasu
City, AZ;
Las Vegas,
Laughlin, NV

Every time I asked a Dolan Springs local where to eat, I was told "Mike & Dee's." I soon found out why. The very tidy, dine-in or take-out restaurant boasts the only pizza in town. Vivacious Mike and Deanna MacKenzie are the restaurant's owners.

Cook Deanna is especially proud of her pizza-makin' capabilities. Townies seem to prefer her Combo version, which is knee-deep in pepperoni and sausage. But her calzones aren't bad either. Deanna stuffs the turnovers with Canadian bacon and sausage. Other specialties are spaghetti, Mexican plates and breakfasts. Arrive early on busy Saturday evenings when the restaurant packs in as many as 35 folks. Not bad for an otherwise sleepy town.

Aside from the giant, angular 25-foot Joshua trees, there's not a great deal to see here. But if you pop your head into any one of the local stores, you're sure to receive a warm welcome. Few towns lie between Kingman and Lake Mead. Parched recreationists often stop at the highway oasis for a bite. Those in the know head to Mike and Dee's.

Tucked inside the elegant Gadsden Hotel is Cattlemen's Coffee Shop. Reminiscent of an old-fashioned soda fountain, the cafe boasts a nearly room-length counter bordered by leather-topped swivel stools. The waitstaff, dressed in classy black slacks and white shirts, serve the house specialties: the stacked Club sandwich, the Mexican platters, and the "sauced" barbecued ribs.

Built in 1907 during the gun-slinging days of Wyatt Earp and Pancho Villa, the Gadsden Hotel served as a luxuriant respite for weary cattlemen, ranchers and businessmen.

Since the days of the Wild West, dignitaries, celebrities and travelers alike have stayed at this National Historic Monument. The hotel's lodestone is its architecture typified by an elaborate, white Italian marble staircase and towering marble columns. An authentic Tiffany stained glass mural decorates a 42-foot wall. More stained glass brightens skylights.

Douglas has several less grandiose but nevertheless historic buildings, most of which were constructed in the early 1900s. Agua Prieta, Mexico is just down the road. You don't need a passport to cross over.

CATTLEMEN'S COFFEE SHOP

The Gadsden Hotel
1046 G Avenue
Douglas, AZ
(520) 364-4481

SPECIALTIES

Barbecued ribs, club sandwiches, Mexican platters

AREA ATTRACTIONS

Slaughter Ranch, Douglas Wildlife Zoo, Cochise Canyon Stronghold; Gleeson, Courtland and Pearce (ghost towns); Bisbee, Tombstone, AZ; Agua Prieta, Mex.

SILVER CREEK STEAKHOUSE

Highway 80
15 miles east of
Douglas, AZ
(520) 364-1341

SPECIALTIES

Quail, rabbit,
Canadian white
fish

AREA ATTRACTIONS

Douglas,
Tombstone,
Bisbee, Tubac,
AZ; Agua Prieta,
Mex.

When travelers venture off East I-10 onto Highway 80, the terrain instantly shifts from desert brown to country green. The two-lane road, which stretches from Arizona into New Mexico, is worth the trip.

About 15 miles east of Douglas, you'll notice a small roadside clearing upon which sits the Silver Creek Steakhouse, owned by Trini and Martha Segovia who reside on the adjoining property.

The large, Spanish-style steakhouse with wrought iron accents, once was a lively cocktail lounge. Today, the pace is slower. A cozy terrace overlooks Mother Nature's panorama. Inside, large windows draw in sunlight, creating a cheerful, tranquil ambience. Patrons pay extra to down savory quail and rabbit, Canadian white fish, and succulent lobster, but every bite is worth the price. Old standbys — prime rib, T-bones and New York steak also are available.

The border city of Douglas, known for the Gadsden Hotel and other historic buildings, is the nearest town.

Picture yourself sipping wine and nibbling gourmet goodies in a plush, pastoral setting. Karen's Wine Country Cafe, situated amidst the Callaghan Vineyards in the tiny community of Elgin, is *the* ideal setting in which to dine. The rambling, adobe-style structure features hand-carved oak tables dressed in blue and white gingham cloths. Oak also trims the large windows that overlook the vineyards.

The Southwestern Sandwich, prepared on homemade cornbread, is a favorite. The hearty, open-faced delight is heaped with Monterey Jack cheese and green chile. Also popular is the farfalle pasta tossed with toasted pine nuts and lemon-herb vinaigrette; the Southwestern Beef Roulades — rolled shaved beef stuffed with chiles and cheese; the tortilla soup and, of course, the wines. Ask owner and chef Karen Callaghan when the next wine-tasting tour is scheduled.

Visit Karen's gift shop next door where she sells her homemade vinaigrettes, sauces and preserves.

The quiet village, located 25 miles north of the Mexican border, was the backdrop for John Wayne's Western classic, *Red River*.

KAREN'S WINE COUNTRY CAFE
Elgin, AZ
(520) 455-5650

SPECIALTIES
Mexican tortilla soup, Karen's Southwestern Sandwich, Southwestern Beef Roulades

AREA ATTRACTIONS
Patagonia, Bisbee, Tubac, Tombstone, Nogales, AZ; Nogales, Mex.

L & B MEXICAN RESTAURANT

695 Main Street
Florence, AZ
(520) 868-9981

SPECIALTIES

Chimichangas,
fruit burritos,
machaca

AREA ATTRACTIONS

Tom Mix
Monument,
Poston's Butte,
Casa Grande
Ruins, Gila River
Reservation

Everything is homemade at the L & B Mexican Restaurant. Owners Luis and Bertha Lizarraga prepare burritos, tamales, chimichangas, chips, tortillas and even *machaca* (beef jerky) from scratch. Frying meats is a no-no at the L & B. "All meats are cooked in their own juice," says Bertha. And Luis grows the fresh, pungent garlic cloves that are used in many of the dishes.

The Lizarraga family is well known in Florence. They've been in the restaurant business for more than 100 years — plenty of time to get the recipes down pat. Fifth generation grandkids Mario and Deana often help out in the kitchen or wait tables. Patrons appreciate the restaurant's lively, festive ambience. The large dining area is outfitted in colorful serapes and sombreros. Mexican theme paintings, created by local artists, hang on walls. Tourists on-the-go take advantage of the cafe's outdoor walk-up, take-out window.

Browse the 100-plus nationally registered historic buildings and the Pinal County Historical Museum. McFarland Historical State Park's old adobe building served as the county's first courthouse and later, as the county hospital.

Siblings Sonny Bracamonte and Marian Horta started out in the restaurant business as pre-teens when Dad opened the El Rey Cafe. At 12, Marian found herself molding dough into tortillas, and Sonny's been cooking "for I don't know how long."

The El Rey closed in 1990 when Dad retired. Sonny, Marian, and her husband, Ed, then bought and renovated an old, run-down bar and christened it (what else?) El Rey. The new business sports a modern Southwest motif and an impressive fireplace.

Retirement didn't seem to agree with Dad, however. He reopened *his* place, which is why there are two El Reys in town. "But the food's great at both restaurants," says Ed at the new cafe. Mexican savories fill Ed's menu but most patrons favor (as I did) Number Five: the enchilada, burrito and taco plate, a scrumptious combo.

The Chamber of Commerce offers historical walking tours of Globe, an old mining town.

EL REY CAFE
Highway 60-70
Globe, AZ
(520) 425-6601

SPECIALTIES
Number 5 — the enchilada, burrito and taco plate

AREA ATTRACTIONS
Besh-Ba-Gowah Archeological Park, Pinal Peak, Miami, Claypool

LONG VALLEY CAFE

Highway 87 and
Lake-Mary Rd.
Happy Jack, AZ
(520) 477-2212

SPECIALTIES

Pancakes, green
chile burgers,
chicken-fried
steak

AREA ATTRACTIONS

Montezuma Well,
Montezuma
Castle National
Monument,
Tuzigoot National
Monument

Thank goodness, we're not expected to serve as chef for the local elk herd," Mike McGuire says laughing. Mike was speaking of the 200 to 300 burly beasts that annually emerge from Coconino National Forest to feed. "Tourists look forward to the elks' summer visit," he says. Mike and friend Denise Knaresboro are proprietors of the roadside cafe.

Travelers also are eager to sample the homemade grub cooked up by the duo chefs. (And, I bet, so would the elk!) Meals are prepared on a free-standing stove inside the quaint, cabin-size cafe whose backdrop is skyscraping pines. Raging appetites are satisfied with chicken-fried steak, green chile burgers, biscuits and gravy, and 16-inch blueberry pancakes.

The cafe is the only commercial property in Happy Jack, population 400. Hikers backpack the trails leading to nearby pristine pools. The nation's second smallest — two-person capacity only — U.S. post office is located two doors down from the cafe.

Jot even owners Eric and Michelle Jurisin know for sure which ghosts haunt Jerome Palace *aka* Haunted Hamburger. The Palace, located in the famous ghost town of Jerome, is nestled on the flank of Cleopatra Hill and overlooks Verde Valley. This lovely two-story building, which dates back to 1908, once served as a boarding house for miners. Restored beautifully by the Jurisins themselves, the Palace features large windows; polished wood floors, tables and bar; and a fair weather deck.

While Eric tends the downstairs bar, Michelle is in the upstairs kitchen concocting the popular Ghostly Hamburger. Cheese, mushrooms, thick rashers of bacon, and roasted chiles stack the juicy patty that locals and out-of-town guests savor.

During its heyday, the hilltop city of Jerome boasted a population of 15,000. But after the mines shut down in the early '50s, most residents packed their bags and headed elsewhere. Others were drawn to Jerome. Its historic setting offers inspiration to both established and budding artists. The town now has more than 500 residents. Unique shops, galleries and museums line its winding streets.

JEROME PALACE aka HAUNTED HAMBURGER
410 Clark St.
Jerome, AZ
(520) 634-0554

SPECIALTIES
Hamburgers, ribs, margaritas

AREA ATTRACTIONS
Prescott, Sedona (Red Rock Country), Oak Creek Canyon, Flagstaff

JUICY'S RIVER CAFE

25 North Ácoma
Lake Havasu
City, AZ
(520) 855-8429

SPECIALTIES
Ranch-style
breakfasts,
smoked baby
back ribs,
homestyle
dinners

AREA ATTRACTIONS
Havasu National
Wildlife Refuge,
Topock Gorge
canoeing,
Parker Dam

What's so juicy about Juicy's River Cafe? It's the heaps of home-made food, tagged at sensible prices. Owners Mike and Sharon Bradley hand-patty ten kinds of burgers including pastrami, teriyaki, and the Frisco version, sandwiched in a Parmesan sourdough bun. Other ribbon-winners include the meatloaf dinner, the smokehouse kielbasa sausage and egg scramble served with biscuits and thick gravy, and the mouthwatering buttermilk pancakes topped with an egg and crisp bacon slabs.

Mike Bradley, once a cattle and land owner, says he knew little about the restaurant business when he opened Juicy's more than 10 years ago. But he says, "I knew what I didn't like — small portions at high prices."

Lake Havasu City is the site of the old London Bridge. Brought from England and reassembled in Lake Havasu during the late '60s, the bridge made the town famous. Visit the English Village packed with shops and galleries. Powerboating, waterskiing, windsurfing, and sailing are favorite activities.

14

Greek eats in a Mexican border town? You bet. Nogales, well-known for its Mexican cuisine, is also recognized as home to a fine Greek eatery, Papachoris' Zulas Restaurant. Owner and chief Chef George Papachoris is responsible for the Greek goodies — notably, the Paithakia Sti Skara platter (lamb chops). But George doesn't disappoint patrons who yearn for Mexican fare. I sampled the beef and eggs-over-easy breakfast plate and the huevos rancheros. Each meal arrives with creamy refried beans and delicious, homemade tortillas. Greek specialties, by the way, cost more than the Mexican dishes but gourmands find the price worthwhile.

After serving as a school administrator for 45 years, George (who had always enjoyed cooking at home) decided to open the restaurant. Wife Tita, an accountant, manages the thriving business.

The Hilltop Art Gallery exhibits local artists' works, and the Primeria Alta Historical Society houses artifacts. Shop for handcrafted Mexican ware in both Nogales' — in the U.S. and Mexico. No passport is required.

PAPACHORIS' ZULAS RESTAURANT
982 N. Grand Ave.
Nogales, AZ
(520) 287-2892

SPECIALTIES
Paithakia Sti Skara, *machaca* and eggs, huevos rancheros

AREA ATTRACTIONS
Tubac, Tombstone, Bisbee, Douglas, AZ; Nogales, Mex.

PAGE SPRINGS BAR AND RESTAURANT

Page Springs Rd.
Page Springs, AZ
(520) 634-9954

SPECIALTIES

Page Springs
Special, steaks,
all-you-can-eat
barbecued ribs

AREA ATTRACTIONS

Jerome,
Montezuma
Castle National
Monument, Dead
Horse Ranch
State Park, Fort
Verde State
Historic Park

Page Springs Bar and Restaurant is a welcome, peaceful respite for weary travelers. The rambling, two-level building sits on the bank of the lovely, tree-lined Oak Creek. Features include wall-to-wall windows, wood beams, and brick fireplaces. The building, a general store in the '50s and '60s, was purchased by Bill and Helma Rohloff in 1974. Son Dan and his wife, Brenda, now serve as managers.

Most diners prefer Chef Rob Secord's Page Springs Special, a tasty medley of beef, ham, cheese, and green chile presented on a hunk of freshly grilled bread. Heartier appetites go for the 18-ounce Porterhouse steak or the barbecued beef ribs. For dessert, try the Pea-Nut Delight, an old family recipe. In area competition, the restaurant was voted number one for three years running.

Page Springs is named after James Page, Sr. who farmed fish in the late 1920s. He sold the hatchery to the state 20 years later. Page Springs Hatchery is located adjacent to the restaurant.

Parker Dam is one of the hottest U.S. spots in the summer. Just check the weather map. Temperatures often soar well over 100°. To cool off, travelers and locals alike escape to Paradise Cafe, a darling restaurant owned by Tom and Laurie Moses. The cafe boasts a warm (cool?), inviting bar and a charming dining area with matching drapes and wallpaper.

Waitress Dawn Nelson speaks authoritatively of the clientele. The cafe, she says, is a favorite hangout year 'round for senior citizens and in the summer, the "water sports" crowd ventures in. The bar has unbeatable happy hours and a savory-sounding menu — half-pounder Paradise Burgers, beer-battered fish, and barbecued baby back pork ribs and chicken. Desserts are homemade and baked fresh daily.

Once you've chowed down, take a free, self-guided tour of Parker Dam, the world's deepest. Next, take a breathtaking, ten-mile waterway drive along Parker Strip, the road between the dam site and the town of Parker.

PARADISE CAFE
Highway 95 at Parker Dam Turnoff
Parker Dam, AZ
(520) 667-2404

SPECIALTIES
Beer-battered fish and chips, slow smoked prime rib

AREA ATTRACTIONS
Lake Havasu (London Bridge), Havasu National Wildlife Refuge, Colorado River Indian Reservation, Alamo Lake State Park

17

THE OVENS OF PATAGONIA

Naugle Avenue
Highway 82
Patagonia, AZ
(520) 394-2483

SPECIALTIES

Stuffed breakfast
croissants,
homemade
soups,
sandwiches,
salads, pastries

AREA ATTRACTIONS

Patagonia-
Sonoita Creek
Preserve,
Patagonia Lake
State Park,
Cave of the Bells,
ghost towns

As much as I love Patagonia, I have to say that visiting the village can lead to disappointment if your timing's not exactly right. This especially is true for Tom Selleck admirers. The last time I happened through, I missed rubbing shoulders with the handsome actor by a week. Selleck had been in Patagonia to film an HBO movie. But dreamy Tom and his troupe are not the only image-makers who venture here. Patagonia, surrounded by grassy, rolling hills and breathtaking wilderness, often serves as a backdrop for photographers and filmmakers.

While Tom was in town, he stopped at The Ovens of Patagonia for a fritter and a mug of coffee. Glass showcases feature a pastiche of mouthwatering pastries. Irresistible to me are the stuffed spinach and whipped cream croissants, salads, and the Cuban soup.

Cafe owners Peter and Aida Maynard brought their Fortune 50 (Yes, 50 not 500!) business savvy to Patagonia two years ago. "We're corporate dropouts," Peter says.

Markets, galleries, museums, and shops line Patagonia streets.

One sign of a well-managed restau-rant is the length of time the staff sticks around. At Creekside Steakhouse and Cafe, Elvera Jones' 12-year tenure is a testament. Boss Olive Matus, who has owned the country-like inn with husband John for more than 25 years, treats her crew and guests just like family. "Some folks have been coming back here for 20 years," Olive says with pride.

The cafe once served as a grocery store and gas station. In fact, the old gas station sign still swings from a towering tree out front. Today, seven wood tables cram the cheery, cozy Creekside. Its windows overlook a dense pine forest. Diners appreciate the vista while replenishing tummies with homemade breakfasts, egg salad sandwiches, and beer-battered fish. Dressings and fruit cobblers are made from scratch. Olive says the Creekside was voted one of the top 100 Arizona restaurants.

The Museum of the Forest houses historic exhibits of northern Gila County.

CREEKSIDE STEAKHOUSE & CAFE

Highway 87/260
Payson, AZ
(520) 478-4389

SPECIALTIES

Beer-battered fish, ribs, steaks, egg salad sandwiches, fruit cobblers

AREA ATTRACTIONS

Tonto Natural Bridge State Park, Payson Zoo, Zane Grey Exhibit, Tonto Fish Hatchery, Mazatzal Wilderness, Highline National Recreation Area

DIAMOND POINT SHADOWS

Highway 260
Payson, AZ
(520) 474-4848

SPECIALTIES

Porterhouse, and rib steaks; oysters, lobster tails

AREA ATTRACTIONS

Tonto Natural Bridge State Park, Payson Zoo, Strawberry (Arizona's oldest schoolhouse), Tonto Fish Hatchery, Zane Grey's Lodge

Look for owner Tony Perna behind the bar when you arrive at Diamond Point Shadows; he'll most likely be standing proudly next to a framed wall hanging of the *National Enquirer*. The tabloid's headline is "Lover of the Year" and guess who's pictured underneath? Tony himself, of course. He's a self-proclaimed gagster. "You should sit here an hour and see my sense of humor work," Tony teases. Perhaps later, Tony. I'd rather sink my teeth into one of your hearty steaks.

Diamond Point Shadows is located on the outskirts of downtown Payson. It's a restful, rustic hideaway, built by Tony more than 30 years ago. Son Michael is now co-owner. The duo sizzle up some mighty hefty steaks — Porterhouse and rib steaks, for example. And from the sea are lobster tails and oysters. Expect to pay extra for these enticements.

At an elevation of 5,000 feet, Payson is a cool escape from the heated valley. But it's a hot spot for fishermen, hunters, hikers and campers. Visit exhibits at Payson's Museum of the Forest.

olks journey from as far away as Mesa to partake of Clark Tatum's Friday fish fry in Pine. Clark, who's owned Tara's Rim Country Cafe since 1989, looks forward to Friday's hordes: "I have a bunch of cooks to feed them all."

The two-room country cafe is managed by its namesake, Tara Rowan. Many patrons opt to dine while seated on one of the swivel stools that hug the long counter. Eggs and bacon represent the choice breakfast, and the homemade pies cause erstwhile dieters to surrender to impulse. Lunch specials are featured daily. Weekends are reserved for the "we barbecue everything" events.

Pine is mountain country. To the north jut the 7,000-foot cliffs of the Mogollon Rim. "Pine's the great escape," Clark says. According to him, many folks from Phoenix own summer homes here. Pine also is a popular getaway for retirees seeking a cool retreat from the Phoenix Valley heat. The antique shops and the Fudge Factory are favorite Pine tourist stops.

TARA'S RIM COUNTRY CAFE

Highway 87
Pine, AZ
(520) 476-3292

SPECIALS
Daily lunch specials, Friday fish fry, Saturday and Sunday barbecue, homemade pies

AREA ATTRACTIONS
Tonto National Bridge, Strawberry, Payson Zoo, Mazatzal Wilderness

21

THE CHRISTMAS TREE RESTAURANT

Woodland Road
Pinetop-
Lakeside, AZ
(520) 367-3107

SPECIALTIES

Old-fashioned chicken and dumplings, beef stroganoff, barbecued pork spare ribs

AREA ATTRACTIONS

Show Lo (year-round resort), Sunrise Ski Resort, Salt River Canyon

I f The Christmas Tree Restaurant is good enough for humorist Erma Bombeck, it's good enough for me. Erma, who has a getaway cabin in nearby Pinetop, often patronizes Omer and Carol Bourassa's cafe housed in a beautifully renovated 45-year-old residence. "The Christmas Tree," writes Erma, "...serves the best chicken and dumplings...I don't like to hurt (the chef's) feelings, I eat some, and some more and some more... ."

Erma isn't kidding. The old-fashioned chicken and dumplings are so delectable they've been recognized in national magazines. "They're my Grandma's 1940 recipe, and we prepare them just like she used to," Omer says. But Omer's entire repertoire, prepared with hand-me-down family recipes, is pleasing. So much so that the menu hasn't changed since the grand opening some 20 years ago. Also popular are the beef stroganoff, barbecued pork spare ribs and honey duck.

The nearby waters — Rainbow Lake and Woodland and Scott Reservoirs — are popular spots for anglers and boaters. Pinetop's forests draw hikers, campers, horseback riders and wildlife enthusiasts.

There are hundreds of reasons to schedule a stopover in Portal, especially if you're a hungry birdwatcher. Nearby Cave Creek Canyon, located in the Chiricahua Mountains, is home to more than 300 species of birds. Annually, thousands of birdwatchers from around the world visit. But studying our feathered friends all day engenders big appetites. When the stomach growlies kick in, most bird hobbyists head to The Portal Store and Cafe for a bite.

Owners Dan and Mary Reece always yearned to own a country store. When they bought the Portal Store in 1987, the deal included a lodge and a cafe. They asked restauranteur and son-in-law Russ Griffiths if he'd oversee the cafe. Affirmative.

The Reeces tend the store and lodge while Russ and wife Devorie whip up the heaped and hot platter creations that include Mexican dishes and lip-smackin' barbecued chicken. Sample the homemade berry-good pies.

The Portal Store sells tourist goods and groceries. Hikers, wildlife enthusiasts, photographers, picnickers, and campers also take advantage of the beckoning Chiricahua Mountains.

THE PORTAL STORE AND CAFE

Pinery
Canyon Rd.
Portal, AZ
(520) 558-2223

SPECIALTIES

Mexican plates, pancakes, chicken-fried steak, barbecued chicken, fruit pies

AREA ATTRACTIONS

Willcox, Douglas, Bisbee, Tombstone

ROCK SPRINGS CAFE

Rock Springs, AZ
(602) 258-9065 or
(602) 374-5794

SPECIALTIES
Hogs in Heat,
Penny's Pies

AREA ATTRACTIONS
Sedona, Prescott

Many entrepreneurs set their hearts on owning their own businesses — but not Jack Exum. Jack decided he wanted to own a whole town, and in 1988 he bought one. After retiring as a TWA pilot, Jack went into the real estate business. When Rock Springs, population six, appeared on a listing, he decided to go for it.

Rock Springs, a city block long, boasts a general store, soda fountain, saloon, and a Western-style cafe and bakery managed and co-owned by Jack's friend, Richard Spain. The restaurant whips up three square meals daily. And on the last Saturday of every month, Richard hosts a "Hogs in Heat" (barbecue) and country music affair. Pork, beef, chicken and mountain oysters are cooked slowly in Arizona's largest mesquite smoker. The bakery itself has quite a reputation. Baker Penny Cooley turns out 20,000 pies annually. That's more than 60 pies per day, which keeps Penny "rolling in the dough" from dawn to dusk. Her famous blackberry pie, cinnamon rolls and breads are palate pleasers.

Rock Springs once served as an Indian encampment and a barracks for miners.

Katy's Kountry Kitchen, adorned with a row of spoked wagon wheels out front, is reminiscent of an antique store. Every square inch of wall, cabinet and ceiling is crammed with you name it — dated U.S. license plates, rusty cow bells, rifles, Route 66 road signs, lanterns, pictures, posters, an elkhead, and on and on. And when it's time to pay the bill, bring along your camera, especially John Wayne fans. Have your picture taken next to the full-color, life-size, cardboard cut-out of the kerchiefed cowpoke.

Twelve years ago, Chicagoans Tim and Katy Lesperance decided to homestead in St. Johns after a vacation visit. And locals are glad they did. Swiss cheese and plump mushrooms top Katy's Alpine burger, and crunchy bacon and yellow cheese crown her Arizonian. Other specialties are chicken-fried steak and Katy's homemade pastries.

St. Johns is situated on the Little Colorado River El Vadito (Little River Crossing). The Apache County Museum exhibits Indian and pioneer artifacts.

KATY'S KOUNTRY KITCHEN
106 W.Cleveland
St. Johns, AZ
(520) 337-2129

SPECIALTIES
Alpine and Arizonian burgers, chicken-fried steak, homemade pastries

AREA ATTRACTIONS
Raven Site Ruin, Kolhuwalawa (Zuni Pueblo), Concho Lake

25

HOPI CULTURAL CENTER

Second Mesa, AZ
(520) 734-2401

SPECIALTIES

Chili Ou-Nga Va,
Noq' Kwi Vi, Ba
Duf Su Ki,
breakfast blue
corn pancakes

AREA ATTRACTIONS

First and Third
Mesas — villages,
galleries,
ceremonies

One way to appreciate the Hopi culture is to sample Hopi native foods. Arrive hungry when you visit the Hopi Cultural Center, a pueblo-style compound that houses a gallery, gift shop, motel and restaurant. The cafe serves compelling, clean-your-plate meals, served by a gracious and attentive staff. Chili Ou-Nga Va is pinto beans and ground beef tossed in a red sauce. The Hopi Taco features fry bread crowned with chili beans and cheese, and try the Noq' Kwi Vi. The luscious stew is peppered with Hopi-grown corn and tender lamb. The Ba Duf Su Ki offers a generous serving of traditional pinto beans along with a bowl of hominy soup. All are the Dawa Na Suf Nova, the Hopi Specialty Luncheons. Many meals arrive with homemade fry bread and honey. Ask to sample the Hopi's unique piki bread. Breakfast and dinner are also served.

The Hopi Reservation itself is divided into three mesas. The Center, located on the Second Mesa, is well known for its silver overlay jewelry, kachinas and coiled baskets.

Take the kids and the "kid in you" to Juan Delgadillo's Snow Cap located on historic Route 66. The food stand, I'm certain, is unlike any hamburger joint you've ever visited. But be advised: Arrive with a sense of humor. Seventy-nine-year-old Juan is, well, a prankster of sorts. I won't reveal his practical joke schemes but be prepared for belly-laughing fun.

The Snow Cap is an eye-catcher. Hand-painted depictions of burgers and sundaes dress its glossy, red-trimmed facade. A snazzy, snow-white, 1950 convertible, equipped with a talking tinseled Christmas tree, is parked in front. In back, modern outhouses are outfitted with — no kidding — television sets.

Snow Cap, circa 1953, is famous worldwide. A German photographer, for example, recently arrived with female models for a revealing calendar shoot. Just ask Juan about the event and his face turns rosy-red. If you're of age (Juan demands credentials even if you're 110), he'll let you sneak a peek at the proofs.

The Route 66 Visitor's Center is just a piece west down the road.

SNOW CAP
Historic Route 66
Seligman, AZ
(520) 422-3291

SPECIALTIES
Hamburgers,
"dead chicken"
sandwiches,
chocolate malts

AREA ATTRACTIONS
Hualapai Indian
Reservation,
Williams Ski Area,
Supai Canyon,
Grand Canyon
Caverns, AZ;
Laughlin, NV

27

HA:SAN HA-SA:GID

Mile Post 91
Highway 86
Sells, AZ
(520) 361-2777

SPECIALTIES
Indian tacos,
chili, fresh tortillas

AREA ATTRACTIONS
Kitt Peak National
Observatory and
Museum,
Sells (Margaret's
Indian Arts and
Crafts Shops)

One hour into the desert, west of Tucson, lies the Tohono O'odham Indian Reservation. Amidst this seemingly endless wasteland is Ha:san Ha-Sa:gid (ha-shan ha-*sha*-gid), a cafe owned by Bernard and Regina Siquieros. Ha:san Ha-Sa:gid, by the way, means "amid the saguaros" in the O'odham language. Acres and acres of untouched sand are peppered with the haunting and beautiful saguaro cactus. (The Indians, I've read, harvest its plump purple fruit. When dried, it's similar in looks and flavor to that of a fig.)

Here, food is cooked the traditional way, over an open fire inside a hut framed by ocotillo (oh-koh-TEE-yo), another desert exotic. Beneath an opaque canopy, diners savor lunch sheltered from the piercing midday sun. My preferred offering is the crisp and puffy Indian taco capped with a mound of luscious chili.

Handmade baskets, such as those fashioned from yucca and devil's claw cacti, are sold at the O'odham-owned Gu-Achi Trading Post.

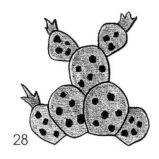

No bones about it — Skull Valley Cafe isn't as spooky as it sounds. In fact, when travelers venture to this tiny ranching community, population 350, *live*-ly folks and decent home cooking await at the local cafe that's been around for three decades. In earlier days, when the railroad ran through the valley, the engineers called ahead to place their orders. "When the waitress heard the train coming, she'd run out with their meals," says Aldona Reid. She and husband David recently became the restaurant's new owners.

Vinyl-topped tables crowd the small dining area that overlooks the Prescott National Park panorama. David is the designated cook and pie maker. Aldona takes and delivers the food orders. But more importantly, she refills coffee cups in a twinkling. David's breakfast of pancakes, eggs as-you-like, and bacon, and his homemade pies are favorites.

Skull Valley itself dates back to 1864. Legend has it that it got its name after a deadly battle between Apaches and Maricopas, which left a trail of skulls behind. Skull Valley Museum, open during summers only, houses memorabilia of the town's history.

SKULL VALLEY CAFE
Highway 89
Skull Valley, AZ
(520) 442-9549

SPECIALTIES
The Breakfast Special — eggs, bacon, and pancakes; pies

AREA ATTRACTIONS
Yarnell, Prescott National Forest, Wickenberg

STRAWBERRY LODGE
Strawberry, AZ
(520) 476-3333

SPECIALTIES
In-season strawberry pies, burgers, marinated chicken

AREA ATTRACTIONS
Payson Zoo, Tonto Natural Bridge State Park, Zane Grey's Lodge (exhibit), Tonto Fish Hatchery, Mazatzal Wilderness

The Beatles' lyric, "strawberry fields forever," came to mind when I entered the charming community of Strawberry. Unfortunately, the strawberry fields in Strawberry weren't forever. With population growth, the buildings usurped the fields. Now, relatively few patches of earth, on which the sweet, wild berries flourish, remain. Yet the Strawberry rage continues. Take, for example, the restaurant that's tucked inside the rustic Strawberry Lodge. In-season strawberry pie is *the* preferred dish. Don't travel all the way to Strawberry without feasting on this strawberry creation. The Lodge also tempts visitors with burgers and chicken-fried steak. Dinner specials are offered daily.

The gem of a Lodge is currently owned and managed by 78-year-old Jean Turner. Her husband Dick, now deceased, ran the place for more than 20 years. Daughters Pam, Debbie and Cindy have served as cooks, maids and dishwashers.

Quaint shops line Strawberry's streets, and Arizona's oldest one-room log schoolhouse, open summers only, is located just down the road from the Lodge.

The surprise in Surprise must be the Rib Cage Restaurant. Hand painted signs throughout this small town lead to the modern building situated in an older residential section. Inside, the spotlessly clean cafe boasts red and black gingham tablecloths, a juke box and small dance floor. Walls are adorned with photos of Magic Johnson, Louie Armstrong, Martin Luther King, and even sweet Aunt Jemima.

The Rib Cage, which opened just three years ago, is "a dream come true" for owner, chief chef, and mother of eight, Unberth Byrd. "Soul food" best describes her hickory smoked fall-off-the-bone ribs and chicken, probably the finest in the area. The barbecue sauce is homemade as are the large blocks of delicious "corny" corn bread and potato salad.

Over the past decade, Surprise has grown into a modern adult community. The Sundome Center for the Performing Arts in nearby Sun City West is the nation's largest single-level theater. The spectacular concert hall, which seats 7,000, often hosts major ballets, symphonies, festivals and popular entertainers.

RIB CAGE RESTAURANT
15808 El Mirage
Surprise, AZ
(602) 583-2012

SPECIALTIES
Barbecued ribs, chicken, hot links

AREA ATTRACTIONS
Wildlife World Zoo, Wickenburg, Cave Creek, Carefree, Fountain Hills (world's largest fountain)

FRONTIER CAFE

Historic Route 66
Truxton, AZ
(520) 769-2238

SPECIALTIES

Chicken-fried steak, deluxe cheeseburgers, home fries and pies

AREA ATTRACTIONS

Hulapai Indian Reservation, Williams Ski Area, Supai Canyon, Grand Canyon, AZ; Laughlin, NV

As a '50s youngster, I often traveled with my Midwest family along Route 66 to visit relatives in California. And just as often, we stopped at the Frontier Cafe for a pie treat. Perched on stools at the long counter, my older and taller sisters propelled the rotating seats by extending their toes to the floor. I, on the other hand, relied on Mom or Dad for a hand spin. I recall this parental indulgence always prompted a squeal of delight.

Frontier Cafe (and Motel) is, as their literature claims, a bona fide Route 66 restaurant that continues to serve down-home good cooking. Mildred Baker has owned, operated, and served as chef for the business since the early 1960s. Relative newcomer, cousin-in-law Jerry Hughes, has helped out for more than six years. Kitchen specialties, Jerry says, are the chicken-fried steak, deluxe cheeseburgers, fries, and still, the pies.

If you haven't traveled the old highway, it's still not too late. There are no glitzy shopping centers, modern restaurants, or fusillades of tourist traps, but the charm remains.

Tuba City Truck Stop isn't just for truckers. In fact, the small diner with 10 tables attracts food mavens of all professions worldwide. The scrumptious, deep fried bread is topped with a heap of spicy Tex-Mex chili, cheese, and a succulent slab of green chile. The recipe is said to have originated in the Stop's very own kitchen. Since the Navajo taco is advertised as the best of its kind in the Southwest, travelers shouldn't leave Arizona without indulging! The restaurant has sold more than one million of the doughy puffs since its grand opening nearly 25 years ago. Local Buck Griffin is the Stop's present owner. Griffin also serves fry bread burgers and chile, and ham and hominy stew.

Tuba City, which pays tribute to Hopi Tribe Chief Tuba, is located on the road that separates the Hopi and Navajo Indian Reservations. The town serves as the Navajo Indian administrative and trade center. Indian crafts are sold at the Tuba City Trading Post and the nearby Toh Nanees Dizi Shopping Center and Van Trading Co.

TUBA CITY TRUCK STOP
Near the junction of AZ 264 and US 160
Tuba City, AZ
(520) 283-4975

SPECIALTIES
Navajo taco, fry bread burger, ham and hominy stew

AREA ATTRACTIONS
Dinosaur Tracks, Elephant's Feet, Grand Canyon, Hopi Cultural Center

CAFE FIESTA

19 Tubac Rd.
Mercado de
Baca, Ste. 9
Tubac, AZ
(520) 398-2332

SPECIALTIES

Spanish black
bean soup,
Egglectable, pies

AREA
ATTRACTIONS

Sierrita Mine,
Tombstone,
Bisbee, Nogales

There are so many artsy shops to visit in Tubac that deciding where to start your tour takes about a lunch hour. I suggest thinking things over at Cafe Fiesta, nestled along the lovely Mercado de Baca strip. Diners elect to sit inside the tiny Southwest-style cafe or outside under an umbrella-topped patio table.

Begin your meal with the house specialty, the Spanish black bean soup and a cool raspberry iced tea. Next, sample the Egglectable. A dollop of cream cheese transforms the traditional egg salad sandwich into a memorable gourmet venture. Polish off the feast with Key Lime pie.

Owner Lynn Greenes also conjures up other homemade delectables such as the red pepper-punched Fiesta salad.

Archaeologists call Tubac "The City of Nine Lives" because of the many and varied cultures that flourished here dating back to prehistoric times. Visit the Tubac Center for the Arts, the Old Tubac Schoolhouse, and Arizona's first state park — Tubac Presidio State Historic Park. Hikers trek the Anza Trail.

Each time I cross the New Mexico border into Arizona via I-10, I think apples — and with good reason. I'm just minutes away from the village of Willcox and Ron and Corinne Stout's Cider Mill. The Mill is the home of delicious, piled sky-high, Granny Smith, four-pounder, $10 apple pies (they're worth every buck!), plus sweet and tart apple cider, and thick 'n creamy apple butter spread.

Pies come in three varieties — Crumb, Classic and waist-watchers Natural, a sugar-free number with a snappy "bites-you-back" apple tart. Other apple tossed goodies are also available, including cidersicles. Feast inside at one of the quaint and cozy booths or request the goodies to be wrapped to go.

Visit Stout's gift shop and view firsthand the cider mill operation. Willcox is home to the Rex Allen Arizona Cowboy Museum, a tribute to the '50s cowboy crooner and movie and television star. Also noteworthy is the Willcox Commercial Store — Arizona's oldest commercial building (1881), and the Wildwood Antique Shop.

STOUT'S CIDER MILL
1510 N. Circle I Rd.
Willcox, AZ
(520) 384-3596

SPECIALTIES
Apple pies, butter, and cider

AREA ATTRACTIONS
Cochise, Tombstone, Chiricahua National Monument, Douglas, AZ

THE COFFEE HOUSE

188 Broadway
Yarnell, AZ
(520) 427-6428

SPECIALTIES
Gourmet coffees, sandwiches, pies

AREA ATTRACTIONS
Wickenberg, Prescott, Jerome

Serious coffee klatching takes place at Gertie Miles' cafe, The Coffee House in Yarnell. Five tiny tables, dressed in dainty lace cloths, fit snugly inside this non-smoking, quaint, black brew and sandwich cafe. (Smokers can light up in a wing located next door.) Talkative Gertie often joins patrons for a cup of the potent coffee.

Gertie's limited but hearty sandwich menu includes the Grotto, a combo of roast beef, ham, and turkey. Other offerings are the all-ham Javelin and the Vegetarian prepared on your choice of wheat or sourdough bread. Soups are popular as are the homemade pies — maple-apple, strawberry-rhubarb, and Mystery Pecan — baked fresh by Gertie's friends.

Three years ago, Gertie grew tired of the Phoenix rat race and moved to this old gold mining town surrounded by desert and distant mountains. "I love it here. There are no traffic jams!" But there *are* shops — antique stores and emporiums that sell local artists' works. Just minutes away is The Shrine of St. Joseph of the Mountains and Yarnell Hill Lookout.

NEW MEXICO

New Mexico is fast becoming the nation's Southwest tourist hot spot. Ski enthusiasts, mountain climbers, golfers, anglers and windsurfers alike revel in its hospitable clime. Travelers are awestruck by seemingly endless blue skies, kaleido-scopic sunsets and dramatic moon rises. New Mexico's breathtaking panorama is one of placid lakes surrounded by dense forests, rugged canyons cut by the Rio Grande, and majestic mountains that loom above the desert floor.

New Mexico's culture is as diverse as its terrain. Three groups dominate — Indians (Apache, Navajo, Pueblo), Hispanics and Anglos. This pageantry of peoples, each with a lively heritage, drive New Mexico's politics, economy and lifestyle.

Learn more about New Mexico by visiting its pueblos, museums and galleries, and by attending its traditional fiestas, fairs and dances. See for yourself why New Mexico is the Land of Enchantment.

CAFE ABIQUIÚ

Highway 84
Abiquiú, NM
(505) 685-4378

SPECIALTIES

Middle Eastern
dishes, New
Mexican fare

AREA ATTRACTIONS

Tierra Amarilla, El
Vado Lake State
Park, Echo
Amphitheater,
Ghost Ranch
Living Museum

New Mexican gourmets are thrilled that Algerian Hassan Segouini selected the Land of Enchantment as his new home. Since his arrival just over two years ago, the master chef has opened three cafes that feature fine Mediterranean cuisine. This one, Cafe Abiquiú, is located in the Abiquiú Inn. The other two, Casbah and the Mediterranean Deli, are in Las Cruces. Each offers similar fare.

Savor Hassan's homemade breakfast granola ladled with creamy, tart yogurt sprinkled with fresh berries. For lunch, sample hummus and the soup du jour (Hope it's spinach on your day!). Then return for dinner to savor succulent baked chicken Algiers or the tender lamb kebabs. Many main entrees arrive with curried basmati rice. Top off the meal with homemade cheesecake and top-notch espresso and latté. Scrumptious New Mexican fare also is offered.

Abiquiú was home of the late Georgia O'Keeffe, who found inspiration for her paintings among the craggy red canyons and the Rio Chama. Visit the Dar Al-Islam mosque.

No, you're not seeing double. El Pinto owners John and Jim Thomas are identical twins. Even when they stand side by side it's difficult to tell them apart. But double doesn't mean trouble. Instead, it means twice the effort, which is probably why the twosome's business has exploded in recent years.

The original El Pinto was built in 1962 by their parents, Jack and Conseulo "Connie" Thomas. At the time, the restaurant seated about 70 people. Since then, El Pinto has undergone 14 renovations. It now seats 900!

Granted, this is stretching the cafe concept a bit, but I have two reasons, besides John and Jim, for including the restaurant. First, the ultra-modern New Mexican ambience, with fountains and lush greenery, is impressive. Second, and more importantly, the food screams homemade.

The twins use the recipes of Grandmother Josephine Chavez-Griggs who built her dish savories upon the native chile. Her grandsons also use the red and green pods in their creative concoctions. The baby back ribs, for example, marinated in sassy red chile seeds, were worth my drive from Las Cruces. You'll see.

EL PINTO
10500 4th St., NW
Albuquerque, NM
(505) 898-1771

SPECIALTIES
Red chile baby
back ribs,
enchiladas,
burritos,
mincemeat
empanadas

AREA
ATTRACTIONS
Old Town
(Albuquerque),
Jémez Springs,
Madrid,
Santa Fe

WILLIE UPSHAW'S NIGHTMARE

Highway 338
Animas, NM
(505) 548-2444

SPECIALTIES

Hamburgers,
turkey and ham
sandwiches,
fish fry

AREA ATTRACTIONS

Birdwatching
in Portal, AZ; Silver
City, Pinos
Altos, NM;
The Pink Store in
Palomas, Mex.

No, Willie Upshaw's Nightmare isn't the title of Stephen King's latest novel. Instead, it's the name of Pat Upshaw's burger joint in the tiny ranching and farming community of Animas. The nightmare, says Pat's daughter Aurora Jensen, occurred when her father Willie, now deceased, began gathering the building materials to construct the restaurant. "Dad traveled to El Paso, Texas and Tucson, Arizona and then hauled the supplies back. It was quite an ordeal. So, when friends inquired as to how things were going, Dad always replied, "Just working on the nightmare."

Later, Willie's "nightmare" became a pleasant haven for locals in search of juicy hamburgers. Experienced diners favor the Willie Burger, a double-fisted, double-cheese number that fills you up half way through — but you finish it anyway. Monday's roast beef sandwich, prepared from Sunday's roast beef dinner, is another winner.

Pat also retails secondhand goods at her New To You Shop. Other Animas stores include auto parts, grocery and gas, mercantile and bakery. That's all, folks.

f I could choose an ideal hideaway, I'd pick Casa Fresen, a wonderful countryfied bakery and delicatessen in the small village of Arroyo Seco. The cheery cafe oozes with warmth. Clearly, owner, baker and former interior decorator Debra Cole has put her heart, soul and earthy talent into this little gem of a place that deserves national recognition.

Dried flowers peek from tiny vases, grandma-style heavy wooden bowls cradle colossal fresh-baked hearth breads, home-canned foods stack solid oak shelves, and imported meats and cheeses tantalize from glass showcases.

Try the rustic sourdough bread ball freckled with sesame, pumpkin, and sunflower seeds, and the classic French baguette. Or, go gourmet with Debra's inventive blend of sandwich fare — the Country Pâté and Chornichon-peppered Gruyère cheese, or the smoked salmon topped with Montrachet chèvre cheese, fresh dill, lemon, and caperberries. Casa Fresen: *un raison d'être.*

CASA FRESEN
Highway 150
12 miles
north of Taos
Arroyo Seco, NM
(505) 776-2669

SPECIALTIES
Three-seed whole wheat and rye sourdough bread; classic French baguettes; green Sicilian and kalamata olive bread; green chile cheese, stuffed croissants; schnecken, gourmet sandwiches;

AREA ATTRACTIONS
Taos, Red River, Angel Fire, Chimayó

LIBBY'S RESTAURANT
203 Hurley Ave.
Bayard, NM
(505) 537-2207

SPECIALTIES
Alambres, burritos, rellenos

AREA ATTRACTIONS
Silver City, Pinos Altos, Hillsboro

Restaurant work begins at an early age in the Telles family. Just ask two-year-old Natasha who wipes tables at what once was her great-great-grandmother's food house, Libby's Restaurant.

The late Grandma Libby bought her first restaurant at nearby Santa Rita Mine in 1949. When a fire destroyed the cafe, she built a new one. Miners stopped by the San Nicolas Cafe daily to pick up their packed-with-love, brown bag lunches. When the mine closed, she moved her business to Bayard.

Grandma Libby, a devoted Catholic, often furnished meals to local folks who were unable to pay.

Today, great-granddaughter Mary Ellen Telles and husband Juan feed the many folks who wander in to the former San Nicolas Cafe. The name was changed to Libby's Restaurant in honor of Mary Ellen's great-grandmother.

Alambres is just one of Libby's winning entrees — sautéed beef, bacon, ham, and chorizo wrapped in a tortilla topped with guacamole and sour cream.

Northern New Mexicans often refer to products of Abuelita's New Mexican Kitchen as "the best New Mexican food around." Now owned by Robert and Anne Romero, the restaurant began with Robert's brother, Chris, now deceased. Chris named the business Abuelita's to honor their grandmother, Perfecta Gonzales.

Four years ago, the Kitchen moved to its present location, an old, renovated adobe home with wood floors and two dining patios. Pottery, kachinas, jewelry and other native artwork are displayed in showcases. The walls are hung with paintings and sketches executed by area artists including Mark Revere and Wilda MacLaughlin. One wall is reserved for a painting of Chris and a photograph of the Romero clan, which includes 11 childen and 28 grandchildren.

Twelve family members work with Robert and Anne to serve such yummies as tasty taco pila (piled high taco), crispy fry bread and crunchy flautas. Save room for the sopa —a sweet bread pudding, or the nattilas — a luscious vanilla custard.

Bernalillo is about 18 miles north of Albuquerque. Visit nearby Coronado State Monument located on Highway 44.

ABUELITA'S NEW MEXICAN KITCHEN
621 Camino del Pueblo
Bernalillo, NM
(505) 867-9988

SPECIALTIES
Taco pila, fry bread, nattilas

AREA ATTRACTIONS
Algodones (Hacienda Vargas), Madrid, Albuquerque (Old Town)

HOTEL CHANGO

Smokey Bear
Boulevard at
Lincoln Avenue
Capitan, NM
(505) 354-4213

SPECIALTIES

Chipotle salmon,
Seafood dish,
Tequila chicken,
veal with
sun-dried
tomatoes

AREA ATTRACTIONS

Cloudcroft,
Ruidoso, Lincoln,
Alamogordo

Don't plan on spending the night at Hotel Chango. The old adobe building, nearly hidden among a stand of sprawling elms, is an intimate cafe. Owner and chef Jerrold Donti Flores named it after his beloved cat.

Jerrold has ingeniously transformed the little space into an exquisite showcase for the antiques he's collected on his world travels. Turkish and Navajo handwoven rugs adorn walls. Nooks and niches contain unusual artifacts such as rare 18th-century Chin Dynasty plates, beaded ceremonial banners, and an early Navajo sandcast belt.

His artistic talents also are brought to "bear" in the kitchen, where he invents delicacies that patrons covet. Popular on the limited menu is the chipotle sauce ladled over poached salmon and the shrimp and scallop dish — seasoned with wine, capers, fresh rosemary sauce and a splash of Pernod. Reservations are recommended.

The visitors center located inside the Smokey Bear Historical State Park shows films about Smokey Bear.

F olks travel far to visit the small town of Capitan, best known as the home of Smokey Bear. But when Spanky's opened two years ago, the focus turned to pizza — *gourmet* pizza, that is. The Chicken Blossom version, for example, is loaded with moist grilled chicken, juicy artichoke hearts and a flavor meld of cheeses — mozzarella, Monterey Jack and cheddar cheese. Weary road jaunters recharge on Spanky's barbecued chicken pizza — plump with tender black beans and tasty green chile and cheese. Spanky's also offers other gastronomic treats. How about a bowl of creamy pumpkin or eggplant soup, or perhaps a crispy calzone? Vodka and port wine lace many of the meat and vegetarian sauces.

Rod Fiddler and Jan Kennedy are proprietors of this casual and unique cafe. They pledge that "the ingredients are fresh, the portions generous, and the price reasonable." And best of all, "we're added at no extra cost!"

Kids will especially enjoy visiting the Smokey Bear Historical State Park.

SPANKY'S PIZZA

101 Smokey Bear Blvd.
Highway 380
Capitan, NM
(505) 354-2234

SPECIALTIES

Chicken Blossom and barbequed chicken, pizzas, pastas, calzones, pumpkin soup

AREA ATTRACTIONS

Cloudcroft, Ruidoso, Lincoln, Alamogordo

LUCY'S MEHICALI RESTAURANT

701 S. Canal
Carlsbad, NM
(505) 887-7714

SPECIALTIES

Burritos, tamales, sopaipillas

AREA ATTRACTIONS

Carlsbad Caverns,
Sitting Bull Falls,
Five Points Vista

I discovered Lucy's Mexicali Restaurant after a ten-mile summer hike in the desert foothills of the nearby Guadalupe Mountains. After the eight-hour trek, I was hot, tired and ravenous.

As I headed to Carlsbad for the night, Mexican grub and a cold Tecate beer were on my mind. I found Lucy's smack in the center of town. The cars parked in front and on the side streets clued me in to what I was to find inside — the aroma of roasted chiles, frying tortillas and carefree, amiable Lucy herself.

As a young mother, Lucy began selling homemade burritos and tamales to help with family expenses. The savory bundles soon became a hit. At the urging of her customers, she opened a small restaurant in 1974. Later, she moved into the present, larger location.

I highly recommend the Super Smothered Burrito — packed with a fiesta of meat flavors and resting in a pool of thick, creamy green chile sauce that's slathered with cheese. Lucy also serves wonderful tasting, low fat Mexican fare.

Stroll the Carslbad River Walk. Visit the Living Desert State Park and Brantley Dam.

The Outpost Bar and Grill is located in Carrizozo, also known as Paradise in the Pines. The village lies in a broad basin surrounded by lush green mountains and foothills.

The dark and cozy Outpost is housed in a Central Avenue building that once served as the town's post office. You can't miss it. Colorful, hand-painted illustrations of burgers and mugs of sudsy beer bedeck its white exterior walls. The business operated as a bar for several years before being sold to Harold Garcia, who added the grill upon which he now cooks his lofty green chile cheeseburgers. I vote his patty as the best in New Mexico.

Harold, who holds double master's degrees in plant ecology and physiology, says there's a science to building a burger: "Burgers taste best when the meat tops the onions, not vice versa." His hand-pattied burgers, two-napkin affairs, are loaded with succulent, plump chile chunks. Also, try Harold's red chile tamale — top-dog delicious.

The Gift Gallery serves old-fashioned malts at their old-fashioned fountain bar.

OUTPOST BAR AND GRILL
415 Central
Carrizozo, NM
(505) 648-9994

SPECIALTIES
Green chile cheeseburgers, tamales, Frito pies

AREA ATTRACTIONS
Lincoln, Ruidoso, Roswell

WHISTLE STOP CAFE
Downtown
Chama
Chama, NM
(505) 756-1833

SPECIALTIES
Farm-bred duckling, fresh fish, traditional breakfasts and lunches

AREA ATTRACTIONS
Santa Fe, Taos, Abiquiú, NM; Pagosa Springs, CO.

Owner Jim Lang had a good reason to name his homey diner the Whistle Stop Cafe. The cafe fronts the head of the Cumbres and Toltec Scenic Railroad, which takes passengers through more than 60 miles of breathtaking Rocky Mountain diorama.

To ready themselves for the long but memorable rail ride, venturers refuel on some of the area's finest food. Jim, a former Santa Fe chef, moved to the historic village of Chama "after Santa Fe grew into an adobe Disneyland."

Jim is locally renowned for his fresh fish dinners including the Idaho trout, the blackened salmon, and the Giovanna-style sherry-sauced shrimp. Farm-bred duckling, cushioned in a homemade honey-almond dressing, is also served. Less expensive, but just as tasty, are the traditional breakfasts and lunches.

Chama is a cool mountain retreat in hot weather. Hike the mountains, raft the river, horseback ride the foothills, and take the train ride. Visit the historic homes and the Fosters Hotel.

ST. JAMES HOTEL

There are strange goings-on inside the kitchen of the historic St. James Hotel. Owner Perry Champion said that one day he was wrangling with a cook about a "less than adequate" performance when a steak knife hurled itself from a hopper and landed squarely between the two. "Enough's enough," the spirit seemed to implore. The cook beelined it from the hotel, saving Perry the nasty job of firing him. But hotel spooks are common at St. James. The ghost stories have appeared in *Smithsonian* magazine, in newspapers, and have been the subject of television programs.

Despite (or perhaps because of) the resident spirits, the beautifully restored and elegant 19th century national landmark remains a tourist attraction.

Reserve a table in the lovely Old West Lambert room, once a late 19th century rowdy saloon. The ceiling still bears the holes that were witness to deadly shotgun duels. Sample the specialty, Chef John Quillman's juicy buffalo steak and the fresh escargot. Other favorites are the Pasta Cimarron and the Chicken Gismonda.

Take a self-guided tour of the hotel (if you dare). Visit the Aztec Mill Museum and the Cimarron Art Gallery.

SPECIALTIES
Buffalo steak, Chicken Gismonda, Pasta Cimarron

AREA ATTRACTIONS
Cimarron Canyon State Park; Taos, Angel Fire and Red River ski resorts

49

COOKSHACK BBQ
Downtown
Cloudcroft
Highway 82
Cloudcroft, NM
(505) 682-9920

SPECIALTIES
BBQ meat and
sandwich platters

AREA ATTRACTIONS
Alamogordo,
Capitan, Lincoln,
Ruidoso, Sunspot

More than 25 years ago, Dale Earthman began serving barbecued platters and sandwiches from a tiny trailer. He named his business Chuckwagon Cafe. A sawdusted tarp in front of the take-out window served as the dining area.

Today, Chuckwagon Cafe, renamed Cookshack BBQ, is located in a permanent structure. Dale's son, Tim, is proprietor. Customers still "wade" through sawdust to get to a table, but they now sit inside at gingham-topped picnic-style tables whose bench seats are propped by hefty tree stumps. The cafe is trimmed with antiques, including a baling wire basket donated by a 113-year-old Native American, who at one time carried it on his burro, saddlebag style.

An old smoker in front of Cookshack BBQ huffs and puffs constantly, curing beef and buffalo meat that later stacks sandwiches. Burgers, barbecued links and sandwiches arrive with beans and "slaw" or potato salad. Ya' gotta' try the buffalo.

Visit the gift shops and the Mercantile General Store to sample homebaked breads and pastries.

Arrive at El Bruno's Ristorante y Cantina before rush hour to guarantee a seat on one of the loveliest dining patios in the Southwest. Indian art, Navajo rugs, giant clay pots, plump pillows, rugged wood beams, and an old shade tree create a memorable ambience.

The Southwest theme continues inside the building. Each dining area is embellished to the hilt with New Mexico furnishings, kiva fireplaces, and chile ristras.

Equally unforgettable are the sumptuous New Mex temptations. Daily lunches, named after area communities, include the Torreon — a plump Navajo taco, and the Regina — tender beans and beef stuffed sopaipillas. Other grabbers are the sizzling fajitas, lush tacos, "juiced" chile rellenos and carne adovada — marinated pork cubes in a red chile sauce.

The cafe, owned by Bruno and Hazel Herrera, started out as a bar 25 years ago. Hazel says many of the recipes are her grandmother's.

Visit the Herrera's adjoining Southwest-style dress and t-shirt shops and the Old West-style cantina. Check out Cuba's visitors center which resembles a thatched roof fruit stand.

EL BRUNO'S RISTORANTE y CANTINA
Main St.
Downtown Cuba
Cuba, NM
(505) 289-9429

SPECIALTIES
New Mex platters,
daily specials

AREA ATTRACTIONS
Zia, Santa
Ana, and Jémez
Pueblos

EMBUDO STATION

Highway 68
25 miles south of Taos
Embudo, NM
(505) 853-4707

SPECIALTIES

Smoked trout and poultry, vegetarian New Mexican dishes, red and green chile beer

AREA ATTRACTIONS

Taos, Taos Pueblo, Angel Fire, Red River

Modern-day Huck Finns and Tom Sawyers will enjoy riverside dining adventures at Embudo Station, 25 miles south of Taos on Highway 68. Embudo Station, once the site of an 1880s railroad stop, is situated on the banks of the Rio Grande. Guests dine inside with a window view or outside under skyscraping cottonwood trees. Enjoy live entertainment and family fun that includes raft cruises, followed by dinner on the patio.

The restaurant is the magnificent brainchild of Preston Cox. He and wife Sandy manage the Station and surrounding acreage that features a microbrewery, an art gallery and a smokehouse where the specialties — Idaho trout, ham, turkey, and game hen — are cured. Open for lunch and dinner April through October, the restaurant also serves lip-smacking entrees such as tender chicken breast marinated in cilantro and olive oil, barbecued ribs and brisket, and taste-challenging New Mexican dishes. Of particular note is Preston's homebrewed chile beer.

A long Española's traffic-choked streets rests the elegant dining retreat, Anthony's at the Delta. Owner Anthony Garcia has decorated the posh establishment with his private gallery collection: oversized Spanish Colonial furniture, santos, Indian pottery and weavings, and the brush work of Santa Fe artists.

The cafe, surrounded by flower gardens and landscaped terraces, was once a neighborhood bar (Delta Bar) built in 1949 by Anthony's parents, Manuel and Marie, and his grandfather Augustine. Since then, the space has expanded and the restaurant and bar have become an intimate evening experience. The high-ceiling, sky-lit pueblo-style cafe is noted for its red chile meat enchiladas. Other selections include appetizers — escargot and shrimp cocktails, and entrees such as the King Crab and filet, the spaghetti scallopino and burritos. The dessert offerings are flan, cheesecake and chocolate mousse.

Take home a treat or a rose from Anthony's adjoining candy shop and flower market. Spend the night at Anthony's equally posh Inn (at least take a peek) located next door. Española isn't far from Indian pueblos and ruins.

ANTHONY'S AT THE DELTA
228 Onate N.W.
Chama Highway
Española, NM
(505) 753-4511

SPECIALTIES
Vegetarian entrees, red chile enchiladas, and burritos

AREA ATTRACTIONS
Puye Cliff Dwellings, Ojo Caliente, Tres Piedras, Taos, Abiquiú

GUACAMOLE'S BAR & GRILL

3995 W. Picacho
Fairacres, NM
(just west of Las
Cruces)
(505) 525-9115

SPECIALTIES

Guacamole-
topped teriyaki
hamburgers, curly
fries, yogurt ice
cream

AREA ATTRACTIONS

Las Cruces, Old
Mesilla,
Stahmann Farms,
Fort Selden,
Elephant Butte
Lake State Park

Guacamole's Bar and Grill is probably the area's most popular outdoor eating establishment. On warm weather evenings, weekend crowds gather in the pleasant courtyard to unwind after the long work week. Piped-in Hawaiian music creats a "luau" mood. Canvas market umbrellas shade tables handcrafted by owner Janis Newman's father, Scott Taylor. Janis and husband George purchased the cafe from her parents in 1988. The property, once the site of a schoolhouse, grocery and motel during the early 1900s, was previously owned by Janis' Aunt Emma.

The family affair doesn't end here, however. George's "Auntie" Jane Wong, a native Hawaiian, supplied the Newmans with her "secret" teriyaki sauce that elevates the specialty burger to best in the West Valley. Order yours crowned with creamy guacamole for an especially "cool" treat on a heated night. Other menu items include chicken-on-a-stick, chicken sandwiches, quesadillas, and smoothies.

The Newmans recently purchased an Italian brick and mortar oven. When it's up and running, pizzas and breads will tantalize. Browse West Picacho's wonderful antique and second-hand stores. Visit nearby La Llorona Park on the Rio Grande.

It's nice to wake up to Something Special, an old-fashioned bakery and tearoom tucked inside a renovated yellow-trimmed home that dates back to 1880. Twenty-nine-year-old owner Dean Barns rises early to create such pastry masterpieces as stuffed croissants, French baguettes, and whole grain and green chile cheese bread. The lunch menu changes daily. (Dinner is served in the winter only.) One day lunch might be avocadowiches or baked moussaka. The next, Baron of Beef or pasta lascala. His charming, down-to-earth mom, Charliene, serves the yeasty and delectable concoctions.

Polished oak floors, doors and tables, and gallery art are featured in each of the three adorable dining rooms — the Main, the Sun, and the one I dubbed the Ivy, which features a window blanketed with the leafy flora. Guests also relax on the lovely garden patio hugged by a sprawling grapevine.

Dean's goal is to create a family-like atmosphere. "I want patrons to feel like they're coming home," he said. And this makes Something Special, special.

Visit gift shops, the museum and the nearby trading posts.

SOMETHING SPECIAL
116 N. Auburn
Farmington, NM
(505) 325-8183

SPECIALTIES
Breads, pastries, gourmet sandwiches and dishes

AREA ATTRACTIONS
Navajo Reservation, Bisti Badlands, Salmon Ruins, Angel Peak National Recreation Area, Chaco Culture National Historic Park, NM; Four State Corners

PAPA JOE'S COUNTRY KITCHEN

Highway 96
Gallina, NM
(505) 638-5525

SPECIALTIES

Two-patty burger,
Mexican
combination
platters

AREA ATTRACTIONS

Chama, Ghost
Ranch Visitor
Center, Jémez
Springs, Santo
Domingo Pueblo

Larry Velasquez had the marketing figured out, or so he thought. He intended to build a video store and arcade next door to Gallina's public school. But once construction got underway, the plan changed. Highway 96 travelers often stopped to ask if a restaurant was going up. They left disappointed when Larry answered "no." Then his neighbors, teachers and students started pestering him. They'd had it "up to here" with cafeteria food, Larry says.

The pleading paid off. Larry and his wife, Lydia, celebrate Papa Joe's Country Kitchen's 10th anniversary this year. "I never thought the eatery would take off, especially in such a secluded place as Gallina," Larry says. The winning dish at the spotless roadside diner is Papa Joe's special two-patty juicy burger. The Santa Fe Opera crowd, which passes through Gallina from time to time, seems to prefer Larry's piquant Mexican combination plates.

The rural community is comprised of ranchers, farmers, and Forest Service and school employees. Hikers often use Gallina as their base camp.

E arthy, country, healthy and friendly define Peephole's Junction, a wonderful getaway tucked inside the gorgeous Gila Wilderness National Forest. It's located across the street from the post office. Proprietor and free spirit Loretta Day, a Gila native of sorts (she's lived here on and off for the past 18 years), finally settled down five years ago, "after my soul did."

All her foods are organic. She enthusiastically supports local vendors, including those who handcrafted the tables and benches, painted the pictures, handmolded the stoneware service, and prepared the dried wildflowers found inside the quaint restaurant.

The breakfast, lunch and dinner menus change daily. A "celebrity" chef, a local of course, prepares the evening meals. A guitarist entertains nightly for a free supper and tips. On my morning visit, a humongous pot of pinto bean soup simmered on the stove top. Freshly baked bran muffins and Mexican corn bread sat temptingly on the counter. Other victuals include quiches, lasagna, and a vegan's Hillbilly Cake.

Hikers, picnickers, campers and anglers pick up supplies at the next door general store before venturing into the dense green forest surrounds.

PEEPHOLE'S JUNCTION
NM 211
Gila, NM
No phone

SPECIALTIES
(menu changes daily)
Pinto bean soup, Hillbilly Cake, Italian fare, breads and muffins

AREA ATTRACTIONS
Gila National Forest and Wilderness Area, Gila Hot Springs, Gila Cliff Dwellings National Monument, Silver City, Pinos Altos

ELLIE'S COUNTRY CAFE

NM 180
Glenwood, NM
(505) 539-2242

SPECIALTIES
Breakfast burritos, stuffed sopaipillas, country-style dinners

AREA ATTRACTIONS
Silver City, Gila National Forest and Wilderness Area, Gila Hot Springs, Gila Cliff Dwellings National Monument

When I returned to my Minnesota home, it was 16° below zero. I just turned around and headed back to Glenwood," says Jerry Pierce, owner of Ellie's Country Cafe. Years ago, Jerry made a visit to the tiny resort town of Glenwood. He was impressed with the friendly folks and the warm weather. To escape blustery-cold Minnesota, Jerry returned to Glenwood for good. Jerry also owns the RV stopover, located behind the restaurant. Not surprisingly, RVers frequent the pleasant, sunny cafe that's decorated with a hodgepodge of homemade crafts, dried flower wreaths and live plants.

Appetites soar upon sight of Jerry's grub. Mine skyrocketed when the breakfast burrito arrived tableside. The giant flour tortilla, trimmed in crispy chips, was chock-full of juicy green chiles and at least a ton of cheese. Needless to say, it was my only meal that day. Jerry also serves stuffed sopaipillas, chimichangas and a bunch of country-style dinners. Baker Maxine Keith is the berry pie maker.

Browse Glenwood's shops for souvenirs. Fish at the hatchery just down the road.

Roasted chiles. I love 'em. Can't live without 'em. For most of the year, I wait impatiently for the chile harvest, which reaches its seasonal peak about Labor Day. And each Labor Day, I travel to the chile fesitival, located in the fertile Hatch Valley, also known as the Chile Capital of the World. The otherwise quiet town of Hatch comes alive with tourists and the sumptuous scent of roasting chiles.

My annual visit to Hatch includes a stop at Rosie's Restaurant, a spotless cafe owned by Rosie Ruiz and husband Carlos. Vivacious and friendly Rosie and her four children work in the restaurant and Carlos oversees the finances.

The *especial* is the Rosie Burrito, packed with pork, potato, chile and cheese and trimmed with sour cream. Equally remarkable is the quarter-pounder chile-spiked burger also a grand way to celebrate the chile reap. Chile relleno fans will appreciate Rosie's — mild pods filled with cheese and topped with spicy beef crumbles, onions, and more cheese.

Visit Southwest and chile souvenir shops.

ROSIE'S RESTAURANT
305 Hall St.
Hatch, NM
(505) 267-3700

SPECIALTIES
Rosie Burrito, chile burgers, rellenos, homemade pecan pie

AREA ATTRACTIONS
Fort Selden, Leasburg State Park, Elephant Butte Lake State Park, Las Cruces

PERCHA VILLA CAFE

Highway 152
Hillsboro, NM
No Phone

SPECIALTIES

Enchiladas, Navajo tacos, baked-fresh apple pie

AREA ATTRACTIONS

Silver City, Pinos Altos, Elephant Butte Lake State Park

After just a few days' vacationing on the road, I always crave a homestyle meal. The last place I seek is a glossy, hyper, fast food joint or a sterile, packed restaurant whose policy is to "get 'em in and get 'em out." Rather, I seek out ma and pa restaurants, like the Percha Villa Cafe.

A full-size teepee out front announces the intimate cafe. Once an army barracks, the building is now owned by 69-year-old "Sweet Barbara" Wilken. Inside, paintings, (deftly brushed by Barbara herself) dress the walls. Four gingham-topped tables are squeezed into the tiny area. One large table is reserved for locals or for anyone who'd like to hear the latest town gossip. This table is *always* full.

I highly recommend Barbara's enchiladas, Navajo tacos, and baked fresh apple pie.

Visit gift shops, Three Angels Bakery (try the chile bread), or sign up for a weekend cooking class at Lynn Nusom's Kitchen.

Intrigued by the teachings and discipline offered by the Zen center in Jémez Springs, Elsie MacKinnon gave up her landscape architecture firm in Boulder, Colorado three years ago to move to this tiny, hilly resort town. Zen notwithstanding, Jémez Springs' main attraction is its hot springs Bath House.

At the time of Elsie's move, the Laughing Lizard cafe was for sale. Needing to make a living, she bought it. The 100-year-old building is refurbished inside with a wood dining room floor, a free-standing stove, and hand painted ivy trim. An adjoining deck, scattered with umbrella-topped tables, overlooks a shady, country-like road. Elsie also owns the adjacent motel.

Elsie refers to her menu as "evolved." Many recipes originated in her favorite Boulder restaurants. Tourist books refer to Elsie's fare as "excellent." Calzones, stuffed with sauce-tossed spinach, cheese and garlic, plus gourmet pizzas, laced with dried tomatos, are favorites. Other tasties include Chicken Zia with chile and the Jémez cheese steak grinder. No one leaves without sampling the chocolate raspberry pie.

LAUGHING LIZARD
NM 44
Jémez
Springs, NM
(505) 829-3108

SPECIALTIES
Gourmet pizzas, calzones, steak grinder, desserts

AREA ATTRACTIONS
Santo Domingo Pueblo, Bernalillo, Albuquerque, Los Alamos

61

CHOPE'S BAR AND CAFE

Highway 28
La Mesa, NM
(505) 233-3420

SPECIALTIES

Chile rellenos,
burritos,
enchiladas,
sopaipillas

AREA ATTRACTIONS

Old Mesilla,
Stahmann
Country Store
and Farms, Las
Cruces, Fort
Selden, Elephant
Butte Lake State
Park

New Mexicans and West Texans flock to Chope's Bar and Cafe, especially on weekends, to celebrate week's end and to nosh delectable chile-inspired chow. The lively cafe, which Longina Benavidez opened in 1940, is an "institution" in this part of the country. Named for Longina's now deceased husband, José Chope, the cafe is currently owned by daughter-in-law Lupé. Daughter Cecilia is manager.

For years, La Mesa farmers gathered at Chope's to discuss agriculture, the weather and politics. Chope himself was a staunch Democrat and served as La Mesa precinct chairman for decades. Later he was inducted into the party's Hall of Fame. Both politics and chiles were heated topics at Chope's.

Today, chile remains a hot issue at the cafe. Chope's is well known for serving chock-full-of-cheese chile rellenos, spirited enchiladas splashed with red chile sauce, and fat meat burritos doused in green chile sauce.

Horseback rides along the Organ Mountains foothills and the Rio Grande are offered by several area riding stables.

L as Cruces is well known for its quality Mexican restaurants, but locals occasionally tire of the "same old stuff." So, when Jesus Duran opened Mariscos two years ago, Las Crucens were delighted. As many townies know, Mariscos means seafood in Spanish, and Jesus lists more than 50 such entrees on his bilingual menu.

Tropical enchiladas, shark fajitas and octopus with chipotle sauce are house specialties. His fish soup is scrumptious. And Jesus' jalapeño pico de gallo and jalapeño paste excite chile aficionados. Other offerings include chicharrón de catfish, crab or oyster; Rainbow trout and whole red snapper. Many of his plate-lickin' meals are punctuated with such exotic savories as achiote, a pungent, rusty-red seed grown in the Yucatan.

When your tummy is full, take a walk through the Branigan Cultural Center, the Armijo House, and the downtown Farmer's Market (open on Wednesdays and Saturdays). Explore the Linda Lundeen Gallery and the Glenn Cutter Gallery. Visit New Mexico State University's Williams Hall Art Gallery and Kent Hall Museum.

MARISCOS
1590 E. Lohman
Las Cruces, NM
(505) 526-8490

SPECIALTIES
Shark fajitas, tropical enchiladas, Rainbow trout, whole red snapper

AREA ATTRACTIONS
Old Mesilla, Fort Selden State Monument, Leasburg Dam State Park, Aguirre Springs National Recreation Area, Stahmann Farms

Las Cruces

NELLIE'S CAFE

1226 W.
Hadley Ave.
Las Cruces, NM
(505) 524-9982

SPECIALTIES

Burritos,
enchiladas,
gorditas

AREA ATTRACTIONS

Branigan Cultural Center, Las Cruces Natural History Museum, Gadsden Museum, New Mexico State University's Kent Hall Museum and Williams Hall Art Gallery

Nellie's Cafe, hidden in a light industrial area in Las Cruces, is where locals have chowed down on delicious Mexican fare for more than 25 years. This family owned and operated cafe originated from an old-fashioned push cart. Each day, Nellie Hernandez (now Quintana) prepared a large batch of burritos for husband Danny. Danny, "the burrito man" as friends fondly nicknamed him, peddled the chile-laden burritos at local auto repair shops, bars, and to seasonal onion pickers. On the first day, Danny sold 15 burritos. Soon after, the number climbed to 200. To the delight of Nellie's fans, she opened a cafe, which is usually packed during lunch hour.

The menu lists all my favorites: enchiladas, chile rellenos, tostados, flautas, gorditas, and tacos. Each platter is bright with cheese, green chile and tomato, and arrives with crispy tortilla chips and hotter-than-hot salsa.

Nellie's daughter, Josie, and son-in-law, Terry Burrow, opened their own restaurant, Little Nellie's Chile Factory, on East Amador. Mom taught the duo well. The food is similarly savory.

Hungry patrons wait in a long but swiftly moving line to place their orders at Ranchway Bar-B-Que. The narrow restaurant, usually packed during prime times, is owned and operated by Jesus and Elsa Rodríquez. The team has been dishing up Mexican and barbecued foods for more than 30 years. Jesus boasts that some of his customers make twice weekly visits. And I know why. The barbecued ribs and pork, drenched in an extra thick, rich and spicy sauce, are a finger-lickin' success. Platters arrive with a hefty serving of pinto beans dressed in a light, not-too-sweet sauce, potato salad that crunches with fresh green pepper, and moist dinner rolls.

But all the entrees are delicious. If you've never sampled caldo, now's your chance to savor the best. It's a spoon, fork, and finger affair. The stew is prepared with large chunks of carrots, zucchini, potatoes, corn on the cob (Yep, on the cob!), and juicy, tender roast beef.

Visit San Augustin Pass, elevation 5,917 feet, on eastbound US 70 to experience a breathtaking New Mexico panorama. Hikers and picknickers head to Aguirre Springs National Recreation Area just south of the Pass.

RANCHWAY BAR-B-QUE
604 N.
Valley Drive
Las Cruces, NM
(505) 523-7361

SPECIALTIES
Barbecued ribs and pork, caldo

AREA ATTRACTIONS
Las Cruces art galleries and museums, Old Mesilla, Stahmann Country Store and Farms, area wineries and microbreweries

EL ALTO SUPPER CLUB

600 Seppal
Las Vegas, NM
(505) 454-0808

SPECIALTIES

Steaks, seafood, Mexican dishes

AREA ATTRACTIONS

Armand Hammer United World College of the American West, Montezuma Hot Springs and Castle, Gallinas Canyon, Storrie Lake State Park

A large figure, donned in a sombrero, guards the entrance to El Alto Supper Club, a kitschy restaurant dolled up in red satin curtains, a diorama Western stage, and a bar gazed down upon by a photo of John F. Kennedy.

Dining is fun at the Club. Before meals arrive, wait staff outfit customers in bibs that match the red-and-white gingham tablecloths. The homemade fare is prepared by 70-year-old owner Judy Domínguez. Foodies go for the chips, burritos, sopaipillas, and the cut-to-order steaks.

Judy began working as a cook in Eddie Domínguez' new intimate nightclub, El Alto Supper Club, in 1940 when she was just 14. The twosome worked well together. So well, in fact, that they married two years later. Today, two of their seven children, daughters Charlene and Macie, and Macie's daughter, Amanda, help out. When Eddie died in the late '60s, Judy took over as owner but continues to whip up meals that receive raves.

Visit the historic Plaza Hotel, the Cultural Center and the City Museum.

Travelers along I-25 often take the Lemitar exit (156) when the stomach growlies set in. This farming and ranching community, just seven miles north of Socorro, is birthplace of the Coyote Moon Cafe, owned by Steve and Linda Steinbach. The former biologists always hankered to operate a restaurant, so when the opportunity came along, they did just that.

Steinbach's menu offers over 130 items not including the "30 different ways we can make enchiladas," Linda says. Offerings are homemade — everything from the salsa to burritos to the barbecued sandwiches to the pies. Kids also are supplied with their own menu, which lists Tommy Tacos, Miner's Golden Nuggets, spaghetti, and of course, enchiladas of their choice. The twosome grow the herbs that season many of their recipes.

On my stops, I've chowed down on the tangy barbecued beef sandwich, the meaty chicken tacos, or the "Killer Burritos."

COYOTE MOON CAFE
Lemitar, NM
(505) 835-2536

SPECIALTIES
"Killer Burritos," enchiladas, barbecued beef sandwiches

AREA ATTRACTIONS
Elephant Butte State Park, Truth or Consequences, Hillsboro, New Mexico Institute of Mining and Technology (Socorro)

STAGECOACH CAFE

Highway 380
Lincoln, NM
(505) 653-4525

SPECIALTIES

Blue corn enchiladas, chili bowl, nacho grande

AREA ATTRACTIONS

Capitan, Cloudcroft, Ruidoso, Alamogordo

Lincoln. A mountain village with a tumultuous past — Billy the Kid, Apache warriors, the Lincoln County War and Kit Carson. But these days, Lincoln is serene. Streets are roamed mostly by history buffs who take the leisurely self-guided walking tour, which includes the old Wortley Hotel. There are no tourist shops or chain restaurants.

Many strollers "break" at the original overland stage stop, now the Stagecoach Cafe and the Museum of the American Indian. The Ficke family — Elizabeth, son Frederick and daughter-in-law Martha — operate both the restaurant and the museum. The original wood floors, carved wood tables topped with lacy cloths, and the impressive cut stone fireplace create the cafe's lovely, turn-of-the-century ambiance.

Menu highlights include blue corn tortillas filled with fork-tender chicken and spicy green chile, the chili bowl topped with eye-smarting jalapeños, and the nacho grande — tortilla triangles decked out in cheese, meat, beans, and black olives. "Billy the Kid" burgers and traditional breakfasts are also available.

The Luna Mansion is a gorgeous Southern colonial-style adobe home situated on a plush oasis of green grass.

Once the residence of the Don Antonio José Luna family in the 1880s, the now-registered National Historic Landmark was transformed into a restaurant 20 years ago. General Manager David Scoville oversees elegance that includes two bars, a solarium and a wine cellar.

Food service begins at 4:30 p.m. in the upstairs bar. Munchies and other "light" fare include spinach-stuffed shrimp topped with spicy Cajun cream sauce and Southwest chile spring rolls. Sample such sumptuous sandwiches as the Jamaican broiled pork loin and the six-ounce Mansion sirloin burger.

Dinner feasts commence at 5 p.m. in the downstairs dining areas, including the Parlor where the New Mexico Constitution is said to have been signed in 1912. Daily specials vary. Offerings may include ostrich, elk, duck and venison. Piñon crusted pork loin topped with red chile cream sauce and fettucine carbonara tossed with pancetta bacon are other palate pleasers.

LUNA MANSION
Highway 6 and
Highway 85
Los Lunas, NM
(505) 865-7333

SPECIALTIES
Exotic meats and
seafood, Mansion
burgers, pasta

AREA ATTRACTIONS
Isleta Pueblo,
Albuquerque
(Old Town),
Santa Fe

69

MAMA LISA'S GHOST TOWN KITCHEN aka NO PITY CAFE

Highway 14
House 13
#2859
Madrid, NM
(505) 471-5769

SPECIALTIES

Stuffed breads, pastries, vegetarian dishes, Mexican chocolate espresso

AREA ATTRACTIONS

The Turquoise Trail (scenic NM 14 drive), Hacienda Vargas (Algodones), Albuquerque, Santa Fe

Ten years ago, Lisa Interlandi was traveling from California to Santa Fe when she took a wrong turn and ended up in Madrid, a ghost town. Madrid, so different from crowded California and trendy Santa Fe, was instantly appealing. Madrid's population, Lisa said, was about 20, most of whom were artists. Lisa rented an old home and set up her pottery studio and gallery. To lure customers, she prepared home-baked foods, which immediately became a hit. Soon after, Lisa transformed the studio into Mama Lisa's Ghost Town Kitchen *aka* No Pity Cafe, the latter so-named after she served a hot chile dish. "Have you no pity?" patrons teased.

Vegetarians (and carnivores) will appreciate Lisa's wonderful hummus sandwiches, baba ganoush and lasagna. Her stuffed breads — brie and garlic, and ground beef are outstanding. And wait until you taste her humongous pies!

Madrid, population 300, has grown into a quaint shoppers' village that showcases local artwork.

ttention Baby Boomers: Visit Evett's Cafe for a blast of the past. Glass showcases display old bottles, radios, adding machines, and what could have been the Brownie camera Mom gave me when I turned 10. Old Nesbitt's Orange Drink posters are plastered on walls.

The cafe resides in what was once the Magdalena Bank Building, as evidenced by the chiseled-out name on the building's brick facade. During the Depression, the bank was forced to close and a former mayor, Red Evett, transformed the building into a drug store.

Now the space is a local hangout, especially for teens and ranchers. When tourists get wind of the place, they drop in for a thick malt (still served in an aluminum container), a mountain of fries, and either the foot-long hot dog or the bulging burger. Evett's Cafe: good, old-fashioned fun and flavors.

The Magdalena library and city hall are located in the renovated old railroad depot.

EVETT'S CAFE

Highway 60
Magdalena, NM
(505) 854-2449

SPECIALTIES

Malts, shakes, foot-long hot dogs, giant burgers

AREA ATTRACTIONS

Datil Well National Recreation Site, National Radio Astronomy Observatory, VLA Telescope

FIRE HOUSE CAFE

E. Highway 82
Mayhill, NM
(505) 687-2267

SPECIALTIES

Flapjacks,
burgers, Navajo
tacos,
homemade pies

AREA ATTRACTIONS

Cloudcroft,
Ruidoso, Capitan,
Lincoln, Carrizozo

After the new Mayhill fire station was built, Linda Madron converted the old one into a restaurant she named the Fire House Cafe. A fireman's hat and a fire hydrant are the only reminders of the building's previous life.

Be apprised that the structure hasn't seen many improvements over the years so the cafe appears, well, run down. It is clean, nonetheless, and plans are underway to renovate.

Such drawbacks, however, shouldn't impede serious gourmands in search of terrific homemade grub. I arrived at the Fire House in time to sample the old-fashioned flapjack, eggs and bacon combination. The massive flapjack, laced with cinnamon and sugar and topped with a dollop of butter, was thick, moist and downright delicious. The eggs were morning fresh and the bacon just as I prefer: lean and crisp. Other tummy teasers include Linda's state renowned burgers, plus Navajo tacos and homemade pies baked fresh daily by Linda's friends. Linda's menus, typed on brown paper lunch sacks, can be kept as souvenirs.

usually celebrate autumn by traveling to Cloudcroft and the Ruidoso highlands. The cathedrals of trees that blanket the Sierra Blanca and Sacramento mountains are aglow with fiery colors. About 16 miles from U.S. 54 on Highway 380 is the village of Mescalero, headquarters of the Mescalero Indian Reservation and home of the Old Roadhouse Restaurant and Gallery.

To find the Roadhouse, take Highway 380 to Old Road and turn left. Drive about one mile. The "signless" rural hideway isn't easy to find. It resembles many of the residences on the street. On my first visit, the slew of cars parked out front alerted me.

The Roadhouse, owned by Henry Prelo, has three dining areas, including a wonderful sunroom that runs alongside the back of the restaurant and faces an old orchard. Restaurant walls are adorned with Mescalero artwork. Henry's mom, Vivian, painted the lovely retablos.

Most patrons order the Old Roadhouse Combination, a bountiful and colorful display of yummy tacos, enchiladas, rellenos, Spanish rice, and the beaniest of refried beans. Another delight is the sour cream smothered burrito.

OLD ROADHOUSE RESTAURANT AND GALLERY
Old Road
Mescalero, NM
(505) 671-4674

SPECIALTIES
Old Roadhouse Combination, sour cream burritos, tortilla chips and salsa

AREA ATTRACTIONS
Cloudcroft, Ruidoso, Lincoln, Carrizozo

73

DOUBLE EAGLE/ PEPPERS RESTAURANTS
On the Plaza
Mesilla, NM
(505) 523-4999

SPECIALTIES
Tournedos
Maximillian,
Shrimp Scampi
Chardonnay,
raspberry
sauce turkey
sandwich,
Mesilla chicken

AREA ATTRACTIONS
Las Cruces —
Stahmann Farms,
Glenn Cutter
Gallery, Branigan
Cultural Center,
Las Cruces
Natural History
Museum,
Gadsden Museum

Two ghosts haunt an old adobe building, circa 1840, in historic Mesilla. Once the residence of the Ortiz family, it is now home of the Double Eagle/Peppers Restaurants. Legend has it that Mother Ortiz discovered her teenage son engaged in, well, a compromising situation with her maid. Outraged, she stabbed the maid (and her son unintentionally) to death. Since then, their spirits are said to raise havoc in the Carlota Salon room where wait staff occasionally discover broken wine glasses and toppled chairs.

Despite the spirits, the restaurants, owned by W. "Buddy" Ritter, draw crowds. Double Eagle guests feast on dinner in the regal Maximillian Room, which is adorned with Baccarat crystal chandeliers and a ceiling leafed with 24 karat gold. Specialties include the tableside-grilled Tournedos Maximillian and the supple Shrimp Scampi Chardonnay. Peppers patrons lunch in the lovely sky-lit garden and fountain room. Favorites are the turkey and raspberry sauce sandwich and the Mesilla mesquite chicken.

Buddy also owns a microbrewery. Try the Dog Spit Stout, which in 1995 received a gold medal from the Great American Beer Festival.

Mesilla Plaza is surrounded by shops and galleries.

Are you in the mood to sip Pinot Grigio wine and feast on scrumptious Italian cuisine in a *trattoria*-like setting? If you are one of the lucky ones who have dined in a *trattoria,* you know that these small, family-owned Italian kitchens serve simple, delicious cuisine.

Lament not if the family budget constrains your foreign travel plans. Lorenzo's, specializing in Sicilian cookery, is located in Mesilla, USA. The owner, ambitious Lorenzo Liberto, describes his father as full-blooded Sicilian; his mother as Irish. "My Grandmother Liberto," he says, "taught my mom how to cook pastas for my dad." Lorenzo spent a lot of time in the kitchen with them both.

A *must* is his eggplant parmigiana, a juicy, tender, meaty slab slathered in a satisfyingly rich tomato sauce laced with the noble cheese. Yummy turnover-shaped bread hunks, engineered for plate mopping, assures a clean sweep. Go the extra mile and try the ravioli — dainty round pillows of noodle dough plump with moist cheese and topped by a veil of delectable pesto spirited with basil.

For a sweet ending, sample Sicily's signature dessert, cannoli.

If you're in the mood to shop, spend the day in Mesilla on the plaza.

LORENZO'S
Hwy 28
Oñate Plaza
Mesilla, NM

SPECIALTIES
Eggplant parmigiana, cannelloni, penne with eggplant, fettucini Alfredo

AREA ATTRACTIONS
Adelina's (chile) Pasta Shop, Downtown Mall Farmers and Crafts Market (Wednesday and Saturday), Las Cruces; El Paso, TX; Juárez, Mex.

MESÓN DE MESILLA

1803 Avenida
de Mesilla
Mesilla, NM
(505) 525-9212

SPECIALTIES

International
cuisine

AREA ATTRACTIONS

Adelina's (chile)
Pasta Shop,
Mesilla; Las
Cruces art
galleries and
museums,
wineries and
microbreweries

Fine international cuisine and wines are served at the acclaimed cafe, Mesón de Mesilla. Charles Walker, who owned and managed the restaurant for 12 years, recently sold the business to Gina and Stanley Grudzinski. The intimate Southewestern- style building features elegant carved wooden posts and beamed ceilings, kokopelli stained glass windows, and lovely wood wine racks and cabinets. Guests are seated in one of three dining areas, including the atrium that overlooks the cafe's plush-with-foliage walkway. Mesón de Mesilla also provides bed-and-breakfast. The private patio and pool area overlook the spectacular Organ Mountains.

Dinner begins with homemade sour-dough bread and pâté. The wait staff, dressed in smart black slacks and white tuxedo shirts, presents the food roster on a menu board — tenderloin beef, Atlantic salmon, quail, veal Oscar, and a variety of pastas dressed in rich, creamy sauces prepared by award- winning Chef Albert Gomez. Lunch is also served.

Bed-and-breakfast guests select one of two entrees. On my overnighter, I sampled the best pancakes ever — lemon/poppyseed — and poached eggs hidden beneath spoonsful of rich Hollandaise sauce.

When Americans think of log cabin homes, Abe Lincoln's rustic birthplace comes to mind. But the log cabin that houses Granny's Cafe is a far cry from Old Abe's. Open beams bear high ceilings and whirring fans. Tables are donned in homey red gingham cloths. Walls are brightened with scenic photography captured by resident Daryl Gilmore.

When husband and wife Johnnie and Billy Nicholson purchased the cafe four years ago, they "fixed it up." They did a heck of a good job. It's become a popular stopover for travelers headed to the mountains for weekend getaways. Daughter Deeann waitresses.

Old Abe also would appreciate the hearty breakfasts that Johnnie and Billy prepare — light, fluffy pancakes with crispy edges, over-easy fresh eggs, thick slabs of bacon, and tasty grated taters. Customers claim that the burgers are the best in the state. Yummy homemade pies keep sweet tooths satisfied.

The Old Wooten Train Station is up the road. The station hosts Friday evening country music bands and barbecues in the summer.

GRANNY'S CAFE

941 E. Highway 82
Mountain
Park, NM
(505) 682-3190

SPECIALTIES

Hearty breakfasts,
homemade pies

AREA ATTRACTIONS

Alamogordo,
Sunspot,
Cloudcroft,
Ruidoso

77

BEAR PAW PIZZA

Downtown
Peñasco
Peñasco, NM
(505) 587-0030

SPECIALTIES

Enchilada pizza,
calzones,
lasagna

AREA ATTRACTIONS

Santa Fe,
Chimayó, Taos

Don't let the bear paw prints that cover the old, renovated building in Peñasco frighten you away. These days, few burly bears linger about. What you do see are tourists waiting in line at the Bear Paw Pizza restaurant to sample the famous Bear Paw Enchilada Pizza.

Owners Tim and Claudia Davis took a "crash course from friends" on pizza making only one day before they opened the restaurant. Obviously, they learned the task well. Folks from afar travel to this quiet village to feast on the one-of-a-kind enchilada pizza, a double thick corn meal crust slathered with creamy green chile sauce, tomatoes and cheese. Only fresh, locally grown herbs and vegetables are used to create the savory deep dish pizzas and Italian dishes.

The couple "discovered" Peñasco while vacationing in Taos. Both are fine art metallurgists whose work is exhibited in the pizzeria and in Taos galleries. The Davises also are restoring a rare-breed '40s theater that adjoins the restaurant.

Picuris Pueblo is just south of Peñasco. Sightseeing information can be obtained from the Carson National Forest ranger station.

word of caution. Beware of permanent Buckhorn Saloon inhabitant Indian Joe. He's the forlorn-looking, leathery-faced fella, donned in long braids and a beat-up felt hat, who's perched on a bar stool. Indian Joe, a mannequin, appears so lifelike that newcomers often have second thoughts about sticking around.

The Buckhorn is a famous watering hole and fine cafe tucked inside the Gila Wilderness National Forest. The building is distinguished by 18-inch adobe walls and hand-hewn supporting timbers.

After a libation or two in the tavern, most guests retire to the dining room, an intimate charming chamber accented with converted gas lights, Indian artifacts and museum-quality Mimbres art. Reservations are recommended. Quail, swordfish and buffalo steak are some of the splendid offerings that cost extra. The green chile-cheese New York strip steak is the house specialty. The sourdough bread, desserts and salad dressings (The honey-Dijon is simply divine!), are homemade.

Melodramas are performed weekends only in the Opera House next door. Visit the church, the trading post, the museum and the mercantile store.

THE BUCKHORN SALOON
NM 15
Pinos Altos, NM
(505) 598-9911

SPECIALTIES
Green chile-cheese New York strip steak, quail, buffalo steak, New York cheesecake

AREA ATTRACTIONS
Silver City, Gila National Forest and Wilderness Area, Gila Hot Springs, Gila Cliff Dwellings National Monument

BLUE CORN RESTAURANT

Highway 53
Ramah, NM
(505) 783-4671

SPECIALTIES

Blue corn
enchiladas,
"H Bomb,"
braised quail with
pomegranate
sauce,
apricot piñon
stuffed turkey
breast

AREA ATTRACTIONS

Zuni Pueblo, El
Morro and El
Malpais National
Monuments, Ice
Caves

Ahh, the power of publicity. Four years ago, cash flow problems caused Lia Rupp to ponder closing her Blue Corn Restaurant located on Highway 53 in the midst of the Ramah Navajo Indian Reservation. Few folks traveled the desolate strip known as the Ancient Highway of the Americas. Lia needed more volume.

One day, a freelance writer dropped in for lunch and was so impressed with Lia's cookery that she decided to profile the cafe in the regional publication, *New Mexico Magazine*, circulation one hundred thousand. After the magazine hit the stands, Blue Corn was ambushed by tourists. Everyone agreed with the writer: "Lia creates a feast for the senses." Since then, the restaurant has been reviewed in the *New York Times* and Lia's moved to a new, larger location, one that includes a gallery and bakery. Diners enjoy meals while seated at Old Mexico-style tables and chairs.

A *must* is Lia's blue corn crab enchiladas drenched in a cream cilantro sauce and the "H Bomb" burger crowned with swiss cheese, red chile sauce and chile piquine, all rolled into a flour tortilla. Reservations are recommended.

W hat you see here, what you say here, what you hear here, let it stay here, when you leave here," the sign warns locals inside Mary Ann Romero's restaurant, Ella's Cafe. The diner, complete with counter and swivel stools, is Reserve's resident hangout.

Mary Ann started waitressing at Ella's Cafe in her early 20s. When Ella retired, Mary Ann took over. Now daughter Leslie Ann waits tables two nights a week and husband Porfila washes dishes, "when I can get him to do it," Mary Ann says with a chuckle.

Mary Ann's dishes are made from scratch. "I make them like I was taught," she says. The meals are prepared using old family recipes. Favorites include chili, sopaipillas, tortillas, and the red or green (chile) enchiladas. "She makes excellent french fries, too," a customer hollers over to me.

Reserve sits at the foot of the Tularosa Mountains. Arizonians headed to northern New Mexico often travel through Reserve.

ELLA'S CAFE
NM 12
Reserve, NM
(505) 533- 6407

SPECIALTIES
Chili, sopaipillas, tortillas, chile enchiladas

AREA ATTRACTIONS
Silver City, Pinos Altos, Gila National Forest and Wilderness Area, Gila Cliff Dwellings National Monument

RODEO GROCERY

U.S. 80
Rodeo, NM
(505) 557-2295

SPECIALTIES

Homemade
breads and pies,
deli sandwiches,
New Mexican
omelets

AREA ATTRACTIONS

Silver City, Pinos
Altos, Deming,
NM; birdwatching
in Portal, AZ;
The Pink Store in
Palomas, Mex.

"Ask about the homely cook's home baked breads," reads a sign on the front of the Rodeo Grocery. The invitation prompts a visit. "I'm looking for the homely cook," I said. "You found him," answers the far-from-homely, jovial Lloyd Mauzy.

For more than 20 years, Lloyd ran the Rodeo as a grocery only. Then two years ago he started serving grub, including homemade goods. He reserved a splinter of floor space from his grocery for diners. "I'll cook everything and anything to keep people from starving to death," Lloyd says chuckling.

Customers entering the grocery are greeted by freshly baked cinnamon rolls speckled with nuts and raisins. Alongside are sourdough and whole wheat bread loaves and pies. Stacked sandwiches, prepared on made-from-scratch buns, include such deli delights as ham, turkey, and roast and corned beef. Lloyd's huevos rancheros and his New Mexican chile and cheese omelets are early bird favorites. When asked if smoking is allowed, Loyd answers, "Yes, across the street."

Rodeo, population 150, was once a bustling railroad town. Drop by the Chiricahua Art Gallery.

Three summers ago, Willie English and her 80-year-old mother, Sylvia Thomas, were so intrigued by a small and shabby century-old Victorian house that they decided to bring it back to life.

Family and friends chipped in to help strip paint from walls and doors, polish gold-plated fixtures, and varnish hand-carved woodwork. While refurbishing the home, Willie discovered, in the crawl space, generations-old toys, which she now displays throughout the precious Pecos Rose Tea Room.

Inside, everything is pink with roses — the wallpaper, the vases, the tea service, and even the wait staff's striking aprons. Eye-catchers include the ornate fireplace and nostalgic gold picture frames that decorate walls. Charming cherubs dangle from ceilings and decorate old-fashioned Hallmark cards.

Everything from the peach-with-a-punch tea, to the chicken on nut wheat bread, to the torte cheesecake doused in raspberry sauce, is scrumptious.

Visit the UFO International, UFO Enigma, Chaves County and Roswell museums.

PECOS ROSE TEA ROOM
709 N. Main
Roswell, NM
(505) 626-9626

SPECIALTIES
Tuna
Mediterranean,
Cucumber
Victorian,
and roast beef
sandwiches,
soups,
berry-topped
cheesecakes

AREA ATTRACTIONS
Bottomless Lakes State Park, Bitter Lake National Wildlife Refuge, Spring River Park and Zoo

CAFE RIO

2547 Sudderth
Drive
Ruidoso, NM
(505) 257-7746

SPECIALTIES

Pizza, quahog
clam, Portuguese
kale soup,
polenta

AREA
ATTRACTIONS

Ruidoso Downs,
Cloudcroft,
Lincoln, Ruidoso

The aroma of bubbling yeast and simmering herbs first lured me toward Cafe Rio. Inside a group of people watched mesmerized as owners and pals Neal Germain and Fred Poulos transformed fist-size dough balls into giant disks, which they flipped and twirled with the knack of jugglers. The duo creates homemade heavenly pizzas as well as superb gourmet dishes.

My three favorites are: The Connoisseur pizza — rich, sweet and spicy with layers of parmesan and ricotta cheeses, garlic, sausage and red onions; the quahog clam — baked and stuffed with minced clam, sautéed vegetables and homemade bread crumbs; and the Portuguese kale soup — clumps of spicy sausage and potato cubes. The chefs also concoct, among many other delectables, Galician-style poached scallops and polenta, an Italian peasant dish.

Expect a wait during lunch hour. It's not uncommon for each of the 10 red and white gingham-topped tables to be occupied. But the wait is worth it.

Parle vous français? No? Cela n'a pas d'importance. It doesn't matter if you don't speak French, especially if you plan to dine at La Lorraine, a charming French restaurant owned by chef Pascale Agnel. The Kelly green canopied cafe is nestled between shops on Sudderth Avenue, a popular tourist shopping stretch in Ruidoso. Dress is casual at La Lorraine.

Upon entering the small cafe, diners are embraced by the French culture. Chandeliers hang gracefully from ceilings, candelabra adorn a small red brick fireplace, wine bottles peer from cozy racks, and silver, stemware, and white linen rest on tabletops. Paintings created with a Cézanne flair (several oils by Pascale herself) decorate walls. Colorful miniature cacti are patrons' only reminder that this cafe's locale is the Land of Enchantment.

La Lorraine stimulates appetites with chalices of champagne or wine, and soothes stomach rumblings with lobster bisque and pâté hors d'oeuvres. Sample the creamy fettucine Alfredo, the eggplant Mediterranean sandwich, or the heavy duty Black Angus ribeye. Christen the meal with the créme rum brûlée encrusted with a thin mantle of caramel.

LA LORRAINE
2523 Sudderth
Ruidoso, NM
(505) 257-2954

SPECIALTIES
Fettucine Alfredo, eggplant Mediterranean sandwich, Black Angus ribeye, veal, quail, créme rum brûlée

AREA ATTRACTIONS
Ruidoso Downs, Carrizozo, Lincoln

MIMBRES VALLEY COUNTRY INN

137 Galaz Street
San Lorenzo, NM
(505) 536-3600

SPECIALTIES

Steaks, Reuben,
Chicken
Mescalero, pies

AREA ATTRACTIONS

Silver City, Pinos
Altos, Santa Rita
Open Pit
Copper Mine,
City of Rocks
State Park, Gila
Cliff Dwellings
National
Monument

For a scenic country caper, travel Highway 152 into San Lorenzo, a small agricultural village 30 miles east of Silver City. Nestled between rural homesteads is the Mimbres Valley Country Inn. The building resembles a home more than a full-blown cafe. Floors are polished hardwood, windows are dressed in lace curtains, and antique hutches and tables decorate corners. During the winter, a free-standing wood stove, heated with cherry wood, keeps diners warm and cozy.

The Inn is owned by the Shirley family. Bob, his wife, Johnny, and daughter-in-law, Wendy, manage the cafe. Wendy's husband, Devin Shirley, is the chef. Devin has spent more than 25 years in the restaurant business. He's fed the likes of celebrities Robin Williams and the Elliot Gould family in five-star California restaurants.

Nowadays, Devin still prepares everything from scratch, including the breads. My favorite sandwich is the Reuben-Rye, which oozes and oozes with melted Swiss cheese, sauerkraut and Thousand Island dressing. Other favorites are the tender Chicken Mescalero and the peach crumble pie.

SAN MARCOS CAFE

O ld McDonald would be envious of Susan Macdonell's "farm" and country eats at San Marcos Cafe, situated along the scenic Turquoise Trail on NM 14. Outside the cafe, patrons are greeted by a flock of penned but honking geese looking for handouts, and the cock-a-doodle-doos of two free spirited pet roosters, "Buddy," who thinks he's human, and his associate, "Jack." The lavishly feathered friends, who have been the subject of newspaper articles, are a hit with customers. Other greeters include a cage of pigeons.

Inside, the atmosphere is a bit tamer but just as amiable. Susan decorates with homespun opulence. The many wares were "accumulated," she says, "from junk stores." A wooden mantel is a gift from a friend, and the hand-carved Mexican tables and chairs were purchased locally. The adjoining sunroom is made cozy with a kiva fireplace.

Susan says friends contributed to her overflowing Rolodex of recipes. She serves a hodgepodge of goodies, including a variety of well-stuffed lasagnas, savory Balkan lamb stew, Greek lemon chicken, creamy quiches, and Eggs San Marcos.

Highway 14 and 22
12 miles south of Santa Fe, NM
(505) 471-9298

SPECIALTIES
Lasagna, lamb stew, quiches, Greek lemon chicken

AREA ATTRACTIONS
Santa Fe, Albuquerque, Jémez Springs

CHAT 'N CHEW

Highway 666
Shiprock, NM
(505) 368-4508

SPECIALTIES
Chile burgers,
hot dogs,
chicken-fried
steak

AREA ATTRACTIONS
Window Rock,
Canyon de
Chelly National
Monument, AZ;
Chaco Culture
National Historic
Park, Farmington,
NM

Cook Lorena Willie is convinced that Chat 'n Chew's thirtysomething grill makes the difference between her burgers and all others. "There's just something about it," she says referring to the zillions of tasty patties that have sizzled there. Indeed, the burgers are both a local and tourist hit. Other grilled favorites are hot dogs, chicken-fried steak, and steak sandwiches.

Maude Rudder opened the dollhouse-like, tree-shaded drive-up nearly 40 years ago. Son Dan and wife Jeanne now oversee the business. During the day, patrons place their orders inside at the tiny counter. In the evening, customers order from their autos. A car horn toot alerts car hops Margie Dan and Lena Pinto. Dine at one of the outdoor picnic tables or chat 'n chew inside your car.

Shiprock, on the Navajo Reservation, is named for the towering volcanic rock formation that resembles a seafaring vessel. Visit the Shiprock Trading Post. Annually in the fall, Shiprock hosts the Northern Navajo Fair.

W hen George Mesa and wife Cecilia opened Jalisco Cafe in 1984, they borrowed money to put in the cash register. "We were so broke," he confessed. But now, the three-storefronts-long restaurant thrives.

Dainty lace curtains and Mexican ware trim the clean, spacious dining areas. Delightful watercolors by local artist Mark Wilson add a festive touch to white walls.

Appetites are roused by the aroma of frying corn tortillas and teased by warm chips and fresh-tasting, sassy salsa. The recipes are from George's mother, Mary, who, in the 1950s, operated the original Jalisco restaurant, named for the Mexico state in which she was born.

Try the chicken enchilada plate — a mountain of tender chicken chunks sandwiched between corn tortillas and crowned with a savory chile sauce, and the bean burrito — luscious refried beans cradled and rolled in a flour tortilla that's smothered in a snappy, memorable green chile sauce.

Yep, there's more to them thar' hills than silver, there's George's place.

Visit the many quaint shops that dot Bullard Avenue in Silver City's historic district. Tour the Silver City Museum, Western New Mexico University Museum, Big Ditch Park and the Old Tyrone/Phelps-Dodge Open Pit Mine and Mill.

JALISCO CAFE
103 S. Bullard
Silver City, NM
(505) 388-2060

SPECIALTIES
Chicken enchiladas, bean burritos, and Mexican combos

AREA ATTRACTIONS
Gila National Forest and Wilderness Area, Pinos Altos, Santa Rita/Chino Open Pit, City of Rocks State Park, Kneeling Nun

STOCKMAN'S CAFE

Downtown
Springer
Springer, NM
(505) 483-2301

SPECIALTIES

Mexican dishes,
Stockman burger

AREA ATTRACTIONS

Taos, Angel Fire,
Eagle Nest, Red
River

It's 6:00 a.m. Locals begin gathering at Martin and Teresa Barrera's place, Stockman's Cafe, an old-time diner. Some patrons elect to sit at the long counter. Others find a spot in a booth or at a table. The smell of fresh-brewed coffee and homemade, frosted cinnamon rolls greet the early risers, mostly area ranchers, I'm told.

Cook Liz Lucero is in the galley readying the grill for the dawn rush. Spicy chorizo platters and fat breakfast burritos are favorites. But so are eggs and bacon. Midmorning, the ranchers' wives assemble for their daily coffee klatch. At noon, lunchers chow down on the "Stockman," a half-pound burger with all the trimmings. Midafternoon it's break time. More coffee, and perhaps a pie slice for shoppers. Dinner. It's the Mexican dishes that lure them. Meat quesadillas, tacos and burritos. Life in Springer wouldn't be the same without the Stockman's Cafe.

Between meals, visit The Brown Hotel, The Corner Gallery and Antiques, St. Joseph's Catholic Church and the Santa Fe Trail Museum.

The village of Tesuque is best known for its wood-carved art and the Tesuque Village Market, where grocery and specialty foods are sold. The Market also features a delightful cafe, owned for more than 20 years by Jerry Honnell. Son Jerry, Jr. is manager. The dining area features wood floors, tables and chairs, Mexican tile, and colorful photo shots of wild animals. Outside dining takes place on the pretty patio.

The cafe, always popular on Saturday mornings, serves plump breakfast burritos stuffed with your choice of home fries, eggs, cheese and chile; eggs and tamale; or pork. But most patrons savor best the famous blue corn pancakes. The ten-inch numbers are dabbled with butter and garnished with a wedge of pineapple and sliced red grapes. The dish arrives with a bowl of fresh fruit — melons, apples, oranges and pears, and a minature pitcher filled with yummy hot syrup. Also noteworthy are the lunch items, including tasty tortilla-wrapped burgers and tender brisket sandwiched between fresh-baked sourdough bread.

TESUQUE VILLAGE MARKET
Route 22 and Bishop's Lodge Rd. Tesuque, NM (505) 988-8848

SPECIALTIES
Blue corn pancakes, breakfast burritos, tortilla-wrapped burgers

AREA ATTRACTIONS
Tesuque Pueblo, Albuquerque, Santa Fe, Los Alamos

CHUCKWAGON CAFE

NM 337
Tijeras, NM
(505) 281-9170

SPECIALTIES

Breakfast burritos,
Brama Buster,
giant burgers

AREA ATTRACTIONS

Madrid,
Chimayó,
Albuquerque

E arly morning, chilly mountain air always boosts appetites. Remedy? The Brama Buster — a castle of homefries capped by a mountain of Colby and Monterey Jack cheeses, juicy green chile and two fresh fried eggs. That ought to do it.

Chuckwagon Cafe, embraced by the Manzano Mountains, is *the* approved dig for locals, hikers, skiers and highway trekkers who arrive with colossal appetites. Plates are hot, heaped and hearty. Besides the Brama Buster, owner Gretchen Lemmon also serves bountiful burritos chock-full of your favorite meat choice and eggs and onions. The plump packages are then christened with red or green chile. Lunchers hanker for the chile "sauced" burgers topped with crisp bacon and melted cheese. Veggie quesadillas are packed with black olives, tomatoes, bell peppers, mushrooms, onions and cheese. No one leaves the Chuckwagon hungry.

Tijeras' claim to fame is a cement plant. The neighboring mountains offer solace to hikers and skiers.

S anta Clara's Cafe could be a picture found in *Ideals* magazine, which specializes in rural America. Homemade goodies abound at Linda Rankins' cozy cafe located in block-long Wagon Mound, originally called Santa Clara. Patrons are greeted by an assortment of made-from-scratch irresistibles — luscious pies, moist breads, frosted cinnamon rolls — invitingly arranged on a cloth-covered table.

Near the end of a "previous life," Linda spotted a "For Sale" sign outside the cafe. She contacted the owner, who agreed to rent the space for $200 a month. Linda obviously has put a lot of love into creating the homey surrounds that make diners feel like it's Sunday at granny's place. The 120-year old building, once a hotel, saloon and barber shop, is a historic landmark.

Sample Linda's pot roast, pork chops or green chile cheeseburgers. Or, skip the main entrees all together — splurge on one (or the whole shebang) of her baked goods. Wow!

Visit the restored (circa 1917) building that now houses the Bank of New Mexico and nearby Fort Union National Monument.

SANTA CLARA'S CAFE
Downtown
Wagon Mound
Wagon
Mound, NM
(505) 666-2011

SPECIALITES
Homemade
baked goods,
pot roast, pork
chops, burgers

AREA ATTRACTIONS
Chicosa Lake
State Park, Taos,
Santa Fe

BORDER REGIONS

The Southwest, by definition, centers on Arizona and New Mexico, but it also includes the bordering regions of Eastern California, Southern Colorado and West Texas. These geographic and cultural cousins inherited their distinctive Southwestern character from Mexico, their kin to the south. Mexico's mix of Spanish and native influences has produced an extraordinary culture colored by its architecture, language and cuisine.

The cafes in these bordering areas are just a hop across statelines. Even crossing into Mexico is easy. No passport is necessary.

AMAPOLA CAFE

218 N. Main St.
Blythe, CA
(619) 922-9472

SPECIALTIES

Chile verde, beef
tacos,
chimichangas

AREA ATTRACTIONS

Cibola National
Wildlife Refuge,
Picacho State
Recreation Area,
CA; Lake Havasu
City, AZ

Originally, I didn't plan to include California in my venture until I met a fellow Arizona tourist who insisted, "Go out of your way to visit Amapola Cafe." I did, and the extra miles were worth it.

The quaint Mexican eatery has been in the Noriega family for nearly 50 years. Ramon and Felicita Noriega bought the restaurant (and name) in 1950. After they retired eight years ago, daughter Elvira, one of their eight children, offered to take over.

The food is homemade. Elvira's mother, now deceased, was a native of Sonora, Mexico, and the recipes are hers. Favorites are the chile verde (green chile) dinner and the beef taco combination platters. Taco combos arrive with your choice of creamy enchiladas, crispy tostadas or corpulent burritos. One customer cast an unsolicited vote for his favorite, the house chimichanga — a large, beef and bean number, deep-fried crisp. Chile neophytes be forewarned: Elvira's salsa is downright hot.

Swimming, jet skiing, rafting and innertubing are favorite sports on the nearby Colorado River. In February, tourists gather to partake in the annual Pow Wow Festival.

isit Steaks 'n Cakes and I think you'll agree that owner Grant Mayfield is a look-alike for veteran television and movie star Karl Madden. And Grant's smile — big, warm and friendly — is just one of the reasons that local civic groups congregate at the restaurant weekly. Lions, Soroptimist, Kiwanis and Rotary signs dominate the diner's facade. "The food's an enticement, too," attests waitress Veronica. She ought to know. Veronica has served the grub for more than 20 years. Clubbers, she says, go for the flour-dredged chicken-fried steak and the beef and pork platters. But the restaurant offers everything from, well, steaks to cakes.

Veronica says that Karl, oops, I mean Grant, is a hard-working boss. "He'd have to be fired first before he'd take a vacation," she says, laughing. The clean, comfortable diner, although spacious, feels cozy. There's plenty of room to seat a mess of tourists.

Water sports enthusiasts play on the Colorado River. Drylanders prefer Blythe's February Pow Wow Festival.

STEAKS 'N CAKES
9026 E. Hobsonway
Blythe, CA
(619) 922-4241

SPECIALTIES
Chicken-fried steak, beef, pork cutlets

AREA ATTRACTIONS
Colorado River Indian Reservation, Parker Dam, Quartsite, Swansea (ghost town), Alamo Lake State Park, Phoenix, AZ

MAMA'S BOY

36th Street and
Main Avenue
Durango, CO
(303) 247-0060

SPECIALTIES

Calzones, Italian
dishes

AREA ATTRACTIONS

Mesa Verde
National Park,
CO; Farmington,
Aztec Ruins
National
Monument, NM;
Four State
Corners

Born with the last name Salzillo, meaning "maker of sauces" (in Italian, I'm told), Jim was destined to specialize in ethnic cafes. His first Mama's Boy is located in nearby Hermosa. The second, a modish Durango restaurant and bar, is located just outside the touristy downtown area.

Jim learned his culinary artistry from, you guessed it, his *very* Italian mom. The build-your-own calzones are based on Mom's recipe. The turnovers are packed with imported cheeses and pizza toppings. Try yours stuffed with Canadian bacon, pineapple, extra cheese, and green chile for pizazz. Then, top it with Jim's delightful marinara sauce. Other tastebud teasers include linguini with clam sauce; eggplant parmigiana, lasagna, braciole — tender beef rolled and packed with garlic, piñon nuts, and herbs; the Arthur Avenue Hero; and dessert delicacies.

I bet that Mama's proud of her boy from the Bronx.

Explore Durango's Victorian downtown. There are plenty of shops to keep you busy all day long. Be sure to take in one of the weekly rodeos.

E njoy a romantic evening under the stars listening to Sinatra at Amore's House of Pasta. Sip Sortori Merlot and appreciate authentic Sicilian cuisine. The cafe, cozy and cottage-like, serves the recipes of the Macaluso and Giordano families. The lovely umbrella-topped patio area, caressed by shade trees, is a prime spot in which to dine on warm summer evenings.

When siblings Charlie and Ernie Giordano opened the business seven years ago, they hired cooks but shooed them away after realizing the recipes couldn't be taught or written.

Meals, Charlie says, are prepared "... just-a like-a mama's. We use a pinch of this and a drop of this and that." The House specialty is cheese ravioli splashed with Alfredo sauce. Other favorites are pasta with garlic butter and the lightly seasoned red sauce that tops many of the pasta dishes.

Pagosa Springs has numerous galleries and specialty shops. Take a historic walking tour of the town and visit San Juan Historical Society Pioneer Museum. Experience a pastry at the Rolling Pin Bakery and Cafe down the street from Amore's.

AMORE'S HOUSE OF PASTA

121 Pagosa St.
Pagosa
Springs, CO
(303) 264-2822

SPECIALTIES

Cheese ravioli, garlic butter pasta, red sauce

AREA ATTRACTIONS

Four State
Corners,
Durango,
Alamosa, CO;
Chama, NM

Trinidad, CO

WHITE SPOT
500 E. Main
Trinidad, CO
(719) 846-9957

SPECIALTIES
Burgers, bacon
and eggs,
smothered beef
burritos

AREA
ATTRACTIONS
Trinidad Santa Fe
Trail Museum,
Baca House,
Bloom Mansion
and Historic
Gardens;
Alamosa,
Colorado Springs,
Pueblo

Vivian Martinez remembers when White Spot's menu items were priced "at most, half of what they are now." Since its debut in historic Trinidad 35 years ago, Vivian has waitressed at this classic diner. Many "charter" patrons still hang out there, but nowadays their grandkids and great-grandkids tag along. The original owners, Bill and Anna Hedegaard, both in their 90s, drop in each Sunday for a homemade turkey dinner.

Resolved to observe tradition, Vivian's nephew Robert Flecksteiner became proprietor in the late '70s. So, aside from the prices, the menu hasn't changed much. Longtime favorites include chuck wagon steaks, chicken dishes, burgers, and hotcakes and eggs. Mexican platters, especially homemade smothered beef burritos, are best sellers all day long.

Even now the torch is being passed. Vivian is training her 14-year-old niece, Erika Vallejos, in the art of waitressing and I bet, scrubbing. This diner receives my vote as one of America's most immaculate restaurants. Everything sparkles, from the circa 1913 cash register, to the original stainless steel swivel stools and kitchen gear, to the shimmering floor tiles.

Here's your chance to say, "I've been to Mexico." Travel west on I-10 to Deming. Take Highway 11 south until you reach the village of Columbus, which lies just three miles north of Mexico. Unlike the car and pedestrian congested bridges between El Paso and Juárez, country hoppers can easily slip into Palomas, Mexico, via Columbus.

Park your car on the U.S. side and walk, in less than two minutes, into sleepy Palomas, whose unpaved streets and walks take you back in time. Palomas has few gift shops but it does offer restaurants. In particular, Casa de Pancho Villa Restaurant and Bar, just one block from the border. Patrons enter the modern restaurant through The Pink Store, filled with "priced right" Mexican ware. Both enterprises are owned by Sergio and Yvonne Romero.

Fountains, greenery, hand-carved tables, whirring ceiling fans, Mexican artifacts, and music create the festive ambience. The menu is loaded with tantalizing Mexican goodies. I savored plump cheese enchiladas drenched in tasty red sauce and the best rice. *Muy bueno.* Warning: the salsa bites back!

CASA de PANCHO VILLA RESTAURANT & BAR
Highway 11
Palomas, Mex.
Phone: 011-52-
1401-60106

SPECIALTIES
Mexican
combination
platters,
margaritas

AREA ATTRACTIONS
Pancho Villa
State Park,
Columbus
Historical
Museum,
Columbus
gift shops;
Columbus, NM

101

LITTLE DINER

7209 Seventh
Canutillo, TX
(915) 877-2176

SPECIALTIES

Gorditas, flautas, tacos, tamales

AREA ATTRACTIONS

Las Cruces, NM;
El Paso, TX;
Juárez, Mex.

Here's a two for one deal. If your clothes are in dire need of a-washing and your stomach needs a-filling, head to the village of Canutillo. Let your clothes spin dry at the Laundromat while the homemade grub next door "twirls your socks."

After Ray Gallegos retired from the post office, he suggested that wife Irene "share" her down-home cooking with the town. It has now been 20 years since the duo opened the Little Diner, also known as the Canutillo Tortilla Factory. (If you have trouble finding the cafe, just ask any local.)

Today, daughter Lourdes Pearson carries on the tradition. Folks travel miles to sample the famous gorditos and flautas. The gorditas, cornmeal pouches stuffed with yummy hamburger bits and cheese and slathered with red sauce, are a tribute to West Texas fare. The flautas, tortillas rolled into miniature-like flutes and deep fried, are packed with shreds of brisket. They make perfect dip-sticks for Lourdes' shameless salsa.

I discovered Cornudas Cafe while on a journey from Las Cruces to the famous Carlsbad Caverns in White City, New Mexico. The desert town of Cornudas is midway.

The cafe has four redeeming features. First, May Carson owns the place (and the six-unit motel and RV park out back). May just happens to be the mayor of Cornudas, population six. Second, a gaggle of baseball caps, more than 400, hang from the rafters. Third, it has a cozy, neighborly ambience. And fourth, the grilled burgers, crowned with fleshy green chile pods and melted cheddar cheese, make Burger King's Whoppers look, well, *very* small.

Adjoining the cafe is a gift shop crowded with handicrafts, notecards and other interesting objects d'art. Annually in May, Mayor Carson hosts a Chili Cookoff. Proceeds benefit the "Reach for a Star Foundation," which helps critically ill children. The cookoff also sponsors a Goose Poop Contest. Don't ask.

CORNUDAS CAFE
Highway 62/180
Cornudas, TX
(915) 904-2409

SPECIALTIES
Hamburgers, fries, homemade cakes and pies

AREA ATTRACTIONS
Guadalupe Mountains National Park, TX; Carlsbad Caverns, White City, Living Desert State Park in Carlsbad, NM

103

H & H COFFEE SHOP

701 E. Yandell
El Paso, TX
(915) 533-1144

SPECIALTIES
Huevos rancheros, carne picada burrito, caldo

AREA ATTRACTIONS
El Paso — El Paso Zoological Park, Old Union Depot, Magoffin Home, Fort Bliss Air Defense Artillery Museum, Border Patrol Museum and Memorial; Juárez, Mex.

As a kid, Dad often took me on Saturday jaunts to a neighborhood cafe for a treat. Perched on one of the swivel stools that lined the short counter, we watched as the waitress fried the fries and churned the malts. All who gathered there knew one another. That's what made it special.

H & H Coffee Shop brings back similar memories. It's a buzz of friendliness and activity. Najib Haddad opened the boxcar-sized cafe (and adjoining car wash) in 1958. Son Kenneth became sole proprietor when Dad passed away 10 years ago.

The short order cooks/waitresses speak only a teensy English. Express your preferred degree of chile heat: *muy picoso*, (very hot) and *un poco picoso* (a little hot). Try the carne picada burrito or the huevos rancheros, gussied up with jalapeños. The plate also arrives with three giant slices of boiled Idaho potatoes and choice refried beans.

To find the Shop, travel east on I-10 and take Exit 19. Turn left (north) onto Mesa St., then right (east) onto Montana. Turn south on Ochoa to Yandell. The Shop is on the corner.

GLOSSARY

baba ganoush. A Middle Eastern dish made with mashed eggplant, olive oil, garlic and lemon juice.

baguette. French bread shaped into a long, narrow loaf with a crispy crust and a chewy interior.

basmati rice. Long-grained, nutty-flavored rice grown in the Himalayas.

burrito. Flour tortilla rolled and stuffed with a variety of fillings such as meat, beans, rice and cheese.

caldo or caldillo. Mexican soup made with beef and vegetables and seasoned with tomatoes and cilantro.

calzone. Stuffed pizza resembling a turnover.

cantina. A small bar or saloon, especially in the Southwest or Mexico.

carnitas. Pork pieces.

chicharrón. Deep fried pork rind.

chile pepper. A green or red pungent pod whose heat quotient varies from mild to fiery. Chile is used as a spice in many Mexican dishes.

chile relleno. A cheese-stuffed green chile coated in egg batter and fried.

chili. Soup made with beef, tomatoes, chili powder, and sometimes beans.

chimichanga. A crispy tortilla stuffed with meat and chile and topped with guacamole, sour cream and melted cheese.

chipotle chile pepper. A very hot chile pepper that can be found dried or pickled.

chorizo. A highly seasoned pork sausage used in many Mexican dishes.

cilantro. A fresh pungent leaf of the coriander plant, often used to garnish and season Mexican dishes.

créme brûlée. Custard sprinkled with brown or granulated sugar, then broiled.

empanada. A Mexican turnover filled with seasoned meats and vegetables or fruit.

enchilada. A tortilla filled or topped with meat or cheese, and a chile sauce.

farfalle. Pasta shaped like bow-ties or butterflies.

flauta. A corn tortilla stuffed with meat fillings then rolled into "flutes" and deep-fried.

Frito pie. Corn chips topped usually with meat, beans and melted cheese.

gordita. Deep-fried pastry pocket stuffed with savory fillings like meat and beans.

guacamole. Dip made from mashed avocados, lemon juice, garlic and seasonings.

huevos rancheros. Tortillas topped with fried eggs, chile, cheese and beans.

hummus. A Middle Eastern dish of mashed garbanzo beans seasoned with lemon juice, olive oil and garlic.

jalapeño. A small hot green chile pod.

lobster bisque. A thick, rich soup pre-pared with cream puréed lobster.

mountain oysters. The testicles of a sheep, calf or boar.

moussaka. A baked Greek dish made by layering sliced eggplant and ground beef or lamb.

nattilas. Vanilla custard.

pico de gallo. A dip prepared with chiles, onions, tomatoes and cilantro.

polenta. Mush made from cornmeal and dolloped with butter or honey.

quahog clam. A large, East Coast hard-shell clam.

quesadillas. Melted cheese and green chiles sandwiched between warm tortillas.

sopa. A sweet bread pudding.

sopaipilla. A puffy, deep-fried pastry drizzled with honey or stuffed with beans or meat.

tamale. Meat and chile rolled in corn-meal and wrapped in a softened corn husk and then steamed. The husk is peeled back before eating.

tortilla. A thin, round Mexican everyday bread made from unleavened corn or wheat flour that is baked on a griddle.

vegan. A vegetarian who eats no animal products.

MUCHAS GRACIAS

• Harold Cousland, editor, *Las Cruces Sun-News* • Marilyn Haddrill, adviser • Traveling companions: my mother and stepfather, Mary and Bill Kimmel; my daughter, Heather Luna; friends, Libby Pruett and Loye Hardee • Jack Swickard, general manager and editor, *The Daily Times,* Farmington • Leia James, communications manager, Arizona Office of Tourism • Jean McKnight, director, public relations, Tuscon Convention & Visitors Bureau • Roberta John, public information officer, Navajoland Tourism Department • Patty Taylor, public relations coordinator, Taos County Chamber of Commerce • Debbie Scott, executive director, Sandoval County Regional Tourism Association • Steve Lewis, public relations coordinator, Santa Fe Convention & Visitors Bureau • Mary Carter, tourist counselor • Mary Kay Cline, vice president of tourism, Albuquerque Convention and Tourism Bureau • Michael E. Pitel, program manager, Heritage Tourism Development, Santa Fe • Priscilla Whitaker, communications coordinator, Flagstaff Convention & Visitors Bureau • Jackie Hunt, executive vice president, Carlsbad Chamber of Commerce • Adelina Willem, owner, Adelina's Pasta Shop • Lynn Nusom, cookbook author • Tonya A. Evatt, photographer • Neil Weaver, past vice president of retail, Outlaws • Ken and Laurie Dahlstrom, owners, Silver Assets • Judy Soles, owner, Diversified Information • Darlene Reeves, proofreader • Linda Harris, publisher, Arroyo Press • Patty Maeder, for being there • Ed Conley, *mi esposo*

INDEX

Index

FEEDBACK FORM

Sunny welcomes your comments. Let her know which places you enjoyed best and least, and your reasons. Also, have you discovered a cafe that should be included in the next edition of *Cafe Hopping in the Southwest*? If so, write it down on this form and mail to the address below, or e-mail Sunny at *CafeHop@aol.com*. Include as much information as you wish: cafe name, owner(s), address, phone number, specialty dishes and your reasons for recommending the cafe.

COMMENTS:

_____

_____

_____

Optional: your name, address and phone number

_____

_____

_____

Need an extra copy of *Cafe Hopping in the Southwest*? Mail your check or money order for $10.95 plus $2 shipping to Arroyo Press, P.O Box 4333, Las Cruces, NM 88003-4333 or call 1-800-795-2693.